The Breaking
of the
Outward Man
for

The Release of
the Spirit

Watchman Nee

**A New Revision, 1999
with a New Study Guide**

Sure Foundation Publishers

*"Behold, I lay in Zion
for a foundation a stone—
a tried stone,
a precious corner stone,
a Sure Foundation..."*

Copyright 1965
Revised, with Study Guide 1999

ORDER FROM
CHRISTIAN FELLOWSHIP PUBLISHERS INC
11515 ALLECINGIE PARKWAY
RICHMOND VA 23235

Contents

Contents

Preface

IN READING this manuscript, we have been impressed with
its vital message and the need to share it and make it known to
all of the Lord's seekers—the ones who long to be channels
for His life. One cannot read very far before sensing Watchman Nee's
longing and prayer for the church to know the Lord in the fullest way.
For this, He must find a minimum of hindrance in us so that He may
be fully released through our regenerated spirit.

Surely, this is an hour when the battleground is over the soul. The
Lord is seeking to work **from the inside**, through the spirit,
regenerated by the new birth. Whereas, Satan is attempting to work
from the outside, through the soul, made corrupt by the Fall. Even
in the believer, the self-hyphenated strengths of the outer man, the
unbroken soul, have not yet been brought under the control of the
Spirit. For this, Watchman Nee helps us to see that in order for His
life-giving Spirit to be released through the channel of the human
spirit, the 'hard-shell' soul of the outward man necessitates breaking.
This is largely accomplished through the dealings of our daily
circumstances which God allows and so orders.

In his many years of laboring with his fellow workers in China, Brother Nee has clearly seen the absolute necessity for brokenness. Moreover, it is almost as if he were personally here upon the religious scene in America where this great need for brokenness also exists among Christian workers. There may be some who are unprepared for such a bitter dose of spiritual medicine. Yet we believe anyone with discernment and hunger will agree that the breaking of the soul-powers of the outward man is imperative if the human spirit is to express Christ as our life freely.

Second Preface, 1976

Rejoice with us! One million copies in ten languages are now in print. In this present hour, when the religious scene is occupied with subjective feelings and emotional experiences, it seems even more important (than twelve years ago when this book was first published) that each one of God's children understand his basic make-up and function of his spirit, soul, and body. For those who are truly pressing for the prize and the upward calling of God, this is indeed a truth most indispensable. We trust then that this message shall reach every part of the Body of Christ and accomplish a release of His life. May it be so for His eternal glory, praise, and honor!

—The Publishers

Introduction

FOR THE READER to properly appreciate these lessons, perhaps a few preparatory statements will be helpful. Firstly, we must become accustomed to the terminology Watchman Nee uses. Following the pattern in 1 Thessalonians 5:23, he uses Paul's statement describing man as spirit, soul, and body. For the purposes of this book, he has chosen to call man's **spirit** the *inner man*. He calls man's **soul** the *outer man*. And for the **body** he uses the term, the *outermost man*. In the diagram below we have pictured this. It will also help us to realize that God, in designing man originally, intended for man's spirit to be His home or dwelling place. So the Holy Spirit, by making His union with the human spirit, was to govern the soul. Then further, the spirit through the soul would use the body as the means of expressing God's life and purpose.

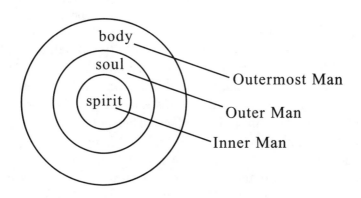

Secondly, when Watchman Nee speaks of destroying the soul, it may seem as if he is using too strong a word—as though he is implying annihilation. Actually, the whole substance of his message clearly points out that the soul is stubbornly independent, that the soul must become the broken organ or vessel for the release of his spirit, and that the soul becomes the functioning channel through which the Spirit of life seeks to flow out. So it is the independence of the soul that must be destroyed, or broken. Then his soul becomes dependent, and his spirit is liberated. As T. Austin-Sparks has wisely pointed out:

"We must be careful that—while recognizing ... the soul has been seduced, led captive, darkened, and poisoned with self-interest—we do not regard it as something to be annihilated and destroyed in this life. This would be asceticism.... The result of any such behavior is usually another form of soulishness to an exaggerated degree.... Our whole human nature is in our souls, and if our nature is suppressed in one direction, she will take revenge in another. This is just what the trouble is with a great many people if only they knew it. There is a difference between a life of suppression and a life of service. The life of Christ, in His submission, subjection, and servanthood before the Father, was not a life of soul-destruction. His was a life of perfect rest and sweet delight. Slavery ... is the lot of those who live wholly in their own souls. We need to revise our ideas about service. It is becoming more and more common to think of service as bondage and slavery when it is really a Divine thing. Spirituality is not a negative life of suppression. Spirituality is a positive life of newness and surplus. It is not the old life striving to get the mastery of itself."

Thirdly, we must see how the soul has to be smitten a fatal blow by the death of Christ as to its self-governing strength. As with Jacob's thigh, after God had touched it, he walked to the end of his life with a limp. His life would illustrate clearly, and be forever registered in the soul, this indelible fact: The soul must never act out of itself as an independent source and never draw upon its own independent resources . Again, T. Austin-Sparks writes:

"The soul as an instrument has to be won, mastered, and ruled in order to submit to the higher and different ways of God. It is spoken of so frequently in the Scripture as something over which we have to gain and exercise authority. For instance, note the following verses:

'In your patience ye shall win your souls' (Luke 21:19). *'Ye have purified your souls in your obedience to the truth'* (1 Pet. 1:22). *'The end of your faith, even the salvation of your souls'* (1 Pet. 1:9)."

Finally, in these lessons we must see why Watchman Nee insists that the soul—the outer man—be broken, be mastered, and be renewed for the spirit's use. T. Austin-Sparks has well said:

"Whether or not we are yet able to accept it as the way of going on with God fully, the fact is that all of the soul's energies and abilities for knowing, understanding, sensing, and doing will come to an end. And subsequently, we will stand bewildered, dazed, numbed, and impotent. Then, we will discover that only a new understanding, only another constraint, and only the Divine energy will give us the strength to keep us going. In such times, we shall have to say to our souls: *'My soul, be thou silent unto God'* (Ps.62:5)—*'My soul, come thou with me to follow the Lord.'* But what joy and strength there is when the soul has been constrained to yield to the spirit. Eventually, the higher wisdom and glory, derived from such a suffering experience, will be recognized as its vindication. Then it is that praise and worship will break forth: *'My soul doth magnify the Lord, and my spirit hath rejoiced in God my Savior'* (Luke 1:46). First, the *'spirit hath,'* and then the *'soul doth'*—note the tenses."

As we approach the end of these lessons, we will discover the secret of fruitful living **unto Him.** Do not fall into the snare, as so many have, of trying to suppress your soul, or of despising it. But be strong in spirit so that your soul may be won, saved, and made to serve His fullest joy. The Lord Jesus has planned for you to find rest unto your souls. And this, He says, comes by way of His yoke—the symbol of union and service (Matt.11:28-30). We shall then appreciate how the soul will see that its greatest value is in serving, not in ruling. True, until broken, the soul wants to be its own master. Thus, it is through the cross that it can become a very useful servant.

—DeVern Fromke, 1965

[Edited quotes from **What Is Man** by T. Austin Sparks]

1

The Importance
of Brokenness

ANYONE who serves God will discover sooner or later that
the great hindrance he has in the Lord's work is not others,
but himself. He will discover that his outward man (soul) is
not in harmony with his inward man (spirit). Both tend to go toward
two opposite directions from each other. He will also sense the
inability of his outward man to submit to the inner control of his
regenerated spirit, received through the new birth. Thus, he is rendered
incapable of obeying God's highest commands. He will quickly detect
that his greatest difficulty lies in his outward man, which hinders him
from using his spirit.

Many of God's servants are not able to do even the most elementary
work. Ordinarily, they should be enabled by the exercise of their spirit
to know God's Word, to discern the spiritual condition of another, to
send forth God's messages under the anointing, and to receive God's
illumination. Yet due to the distractions of the outward man, their

spirit does not seem to function properly. It is basically because their outward man has never been dealt with. For this reason, excitement in revivals, pleading prayers, and zealous activities are but a waste of time. As we shall see, only one kind of basic dealing can enable man to be useful before God—**brokenness**.

The Inward Man and the Outward Man

Notice how the Bible separates man into two parts: *"For I delight in the law of God according to the **inward man**"* (Rom. 7:22). Our inward man delights in the Law of God. *"To be strengthened with power by his Spirit in the **inner man**"* (Eph. 3:16). And Paul also tells us, *"But if indeed our **outward man** is consumed, yet the **inward man** is renewed day by day"* (2 Cor. 4:16).

First of all, when God comes to indwell us by His Spirit with His life and power, He comes into our **spirit** at the time when we were born again (Jn. 3:6). This regenerated spirit located at the center of man's being is what we call the inward man.

Secondly, outside the sphere of this inward man indwelt by God is the soul. Its functions are our thoughts, emotions, and will.

Thirdly, the outermost man is our physical **body**, characterized by its external instincts of sight, sound, smell, taste, and touch.

We thus will speak of the spirit as the **inward man**, the soul as the **outer man**, and the body as the **outermost man**. We must never forget that our inward man is the human spirit where God dwells, the place where the Spirit of the Lord is joined to our spirit (1 Cor. 6:17). Just as we are dressed in our clothing, so our inward man wears an outward man—i.e., our spirit wears the soul. Moreover, the spirit and soul similarly wear the body. It is quite evident that men are generally more conscious of the outer man and the outermost man, but they hardly recognize or understand their inner man, their spirit.

We must know that he who can work for God is the one whose inward man can be released. The basic difficulty of a servant of God lies in the failure of his inward man to break through his outward man. Therefore, we must recognize before God that the first difficulty to our work is not in others, but in ourselves. Our spirit seems to be wrapped in a covering which cannot easily break forth. If we have never learned how to release our inward man by breaking through the outward man, we are not able to serve. Nothing can so hinder us as this outward man. Whether our works are fruitful or not depends upon whether our outward man has been broken by the Lord so that the inward man can pass through this brokenness and come forth. This, in a statement, specifies the basic problem. The Lord wants to break our outward man in order for the inward man to have a way out. When the inward man is released, both unbelievers and other Christians will be blessed.

Nature Has Its Way of Breaking

The Lord Jesus tells us in John 12: *"Except the grain of wheat falling into the ground die, it abides alone; but if it die, it bears much fruit"* (v. 24). Life is within the grain of wheat. But there is a shell, a very hard shell on the outside. As long as the shell is not split open, the wheat cannot sprout and grow. *"Except the grain of wheat falling into the ground die...."* What is this death? It is the cracking open of the shell through temperature and humidity working together in the soil. Once the shell of the husk is split open, the wheat begins to grow. So the question here is not whether life exists inside the shell, but whether the shell on the outside is cracked open.

The Scripture continues by saying, *"He that loves his life* (Greek 'psuche'— 'soul') *shall lose it, and he that hates his life* (Greek 'psuche'— 'soul') *in this world shall keep it to life eternal"* (v. 25). The Lord shows us here that the outer shell is our own life, identified as our soul life, while the life within is the eternal life which He has given to us. To allow the inner life to come forth, it is imperative that the outward life be replaced. Should the outward remain unbroken, the inward would never be able to come forth.

It is necessary (in this writing) that we direct these words to that group of people who has the Lord's life. Among those who possess the life of the Lord, they can be found in two distinct conditions: One includes those in whom life is confined, restricted, imprisoned, and unable to come forth. The other includes those in whom the Lord has forged a way out, and life is thus released through them.

The question is not how thus to obtain life, but rather how to allow this life to come forth. When we say 'we need the Lord to break us,' this is not merely a style of speaking, nor is it only a doctrine. It is most vital that the Lord breaks us. It is not that the Lord's life cannot cover the earth, but rather we imprison His life. It is not that the Lord cannot bless the church, but that the Lord's life is so confined within us, nothing is flowing forth. If the outward man remains unbroken, we can never be a blessing to His church. And we cannot expect the Lord to bless the Word of God through us!

The Alabaster Box Must Be Broken

The Bible speaks of *"alabaster vial of very costly perfume of pure spikenard"* (Mark 14:3). God purposely used this term *"pure"* in His Word to show that it is truly spiritual. But if the alabaster box is not broken, the pure spikenard will not flow forth. Strange to say, many are still treasuring the alabaster box, thinking that its value exceeds that of the ointment. Many think that their outward man is more precious than their inward man. This becomes the problem confronting the church. One will treasure his cleverness, thinking he is quite important. Another will treasure his own emotions, esteeming himself to be more advanced than other people. Others highly regard themselves, because they feel they are better than others, their eloquence surpasses that of others, or their quickness of action and exactness of judgment are superior, and so forth.

However, we are not antique collectors. Nor are we "vase" admirers. We should be those who desire to smell only the fragrance of the ointment. Without the breaking of the outward, the inward fragrance will not come forth. Hence, not only do we individually have no flowing out, but also the church has no living way. Why then should we hold our outward man to be so precious, especially if the outward only **contains** the fragrance, instead of **releasing** the fragrance?

The Holy Spirit has not ceased working. He makes sure one event after another and one difficulty after another come to us. These disciplinary workings of the Holy Spirit have but one purpose—to break our outward man so that our inward man may come through. Yet here is our difficulty—we fret over trifles, we murmur at small losses, and we complain about insignificant things. The Lord is ever finding and preparing a way in order to use us. Yet when His hand slightly touches us, we begin to feel unhappy—even to the extent of quarreling with God and having a negative attitude. Since the time when we were saved, we have been touched by the Lord many times in various ways—all with the purpose of breaking our outward man. Whether we are conscious of it or not, the aim of the Lord is to break this stubborn vessel called our outward man.

Nevertheless, the Treasure is in the earthen vessel (2 Cor. 4:7). But if the earthen vessel cannot be broken, who can see the Treasure within? Have we seen what is the final objective of the Lord's working in our lives? It is to break open this earthen vessel (2 Cor.4:7), to burst open our alabaster box (Mark 14:3), to crack open our shell (Jn. 12:24). The Lord longs to find a way to bless the world through those who belong to Him. Brokenness is the way of blessing, the way of fragrance, the way of fruitfulness. But, it is also a path sprinkled with 'blood from our wounds.' Yes, there is blood from the many wounds we suffer. When we offer ourselves to the Lord for His service, we cannot afford to be lenient and spare ourselves. We must allow the Lord to crack open our outward man utterly so that He may find a way out for His working through us.

Each of us must find out for himself personally what is the mind of the Lord in his life. It is a most lamentable fact that many do not know what is the Lord's mind or intention for their lives. How much they need Him to open their eyes, to see that everything which comes into their lives can be meaningful. The Lord has not wasted even one thing. To understand the Lord's purpose is to see very clearly that He is aiming at a single objective, and it is simply this—the breaking of our outward man.

However, too many of us, even before the Lord raises a hand, are already upset. Oh, we must realize that all life's experiences, troubles, and trials which the Lord sends are for our highest good. We cannot expect the Lord to give anything better, for these constant difficulties are His best. Should one approach the Lord and pray, saying, "O Lord, please let me choose the best thing for my life," I believe the Lord would tell him, "What I have given you is the best—your daily trials are for your greatest profit." So God's motive behind all the things He has ordered for our lives is clearly for the breaking of our outward man. Once this occurs, and our spirit can come forth, we will be enabled to exercise and release our spirit consistently.

The Timing in Our Brokenness

The Lord employs two different means to break our outward man. One is gradual. The other is sudden. To some, the Lord gives a sudden breaking, followed by a gradual one. With others, the Lord arranges constant daily trials, until one day He brings about a large-scale breaking. If it is not the sudden first and then the gradual, then it is the gradual followed by the sudden. It would seem the Lord usually spends several years upon most of us before He can accomplish this work of breaking.

The timing is in His hand. We cannot shorten the time, though we certainly can prolong it. In some lives, the Lord is able to accomplish this work after a few years of dealing. In others, it is evident that after ten or twenty years, the work is still unfinished. This kind of delay is most serious! Nothing is more grievous than wasting God's time. How often the church is also hindered! We can preach by using our mind, and we can stir others by using our emotions. But if we do not know how to use our spirit, the Spirit of God cannot touch people through us. This loss is so great. Should we needlessly prolong the time?

Therefore, if we have never wholly and intelligently consecrated ourselves to the Lord, let us do so now, saying: "Lord, for the future of the church, for the future of the gospel, for Thy way, and also for my own life, I offer myself without condition, without reservation, into Your hands. Lord, I **delight** to offer myself unto You, and I'm willing to let You have Your full way through me."

The Meaning of the Cross

Often we hear about the cross.[1] Perhaps we are too familiar with the term. But what is the cross after all? We shall see it means the breaking of the outward man. The cross reduces the outward man to

---

[1]

The cross has several facets. After first realizing by faith the position of our identification with Christ's death and resurrection, we then begin to walk daily on the pathway of the cross. Without basing the pathway upon the position, we shall be plunged into confusion and self-effort. For further clarification, read **The Normal Christian Life** by the author. It is an excellent pre-requisite to this volume. —Ed.

death. It splits open the human shell. The cross must break all that belongs to our outward man—our opinions, our ways, our cleverness, our self-love, our selfish interests, our all. Clearly, this is the Lord's way. In fact, it's crystal clear.

As soon as our outward man is broken, our spirit can easily come forth. Consider a brother as an example. All who know him will acknowledge that he has a keen mind, a decisive will, and refined emotions. But instead of being impressed by the natural characteristics of his soul, they realize they have met his spirit. Whenever people fellowship with him, they encounter a released and a transparent spirit. Why? Because everything characterizing the soul of his outward man has been dealt with.

Take a sister as another example. Those who know her recognize her quick disposition. She is quick in thought, quick of speech, quick to confess, quick in writing letters, and quick to tear up what she has written. However, those who meet her do not meet her quickness. Instead, they touch the flowing out of her spirit. She is one who has been utterly broken and has become transparent. This breaking of the outward man is very basic. We should not cling to our weak, soulish characteristics, still emitting the same old natural discharges after five or ten years of the Lord's dealing. No, it is important to allow the Lord to forge a way out through the hard shell of our outward man.

Two Reasons for Not Being Broken

Why is it that after many years under the Lord's dealing, some remain the same? Some individuals have a forceful will. Many have powerful emotions. And others have a strong mind. Since the Lord is able to break these, why is it, after so many years, some are still unchanged? We believe there are two main reasons.

First, they live in **darkness**. Hence, they do not see the hand of God. While God is working, while God is attempting to break their

18

natural, soulish strengths, they do not recognize it as being from Him. They are devoid of light, seeing only men opposing them. They imagine their environment is just too difficult, and their circumstances are to blame. So they linger in their darkness and despair.

May God give us enlightenment to see what is from His hand. Subsequently, may we kneel down and say to Him, "It is You after all. Since it is You, I will accept what You are doing." At least, we must recognize **Whose** hand is dealing with us. It is not a human hand. Nor is it our family's hand. It's not the brothers and sisters' hand in the church. But it is God's very own hand that is dealing with us. We need to learn how to kneel down, kiss the hand, and love the hand that deals with us, even as Madame Guyon did. We must have this kind of light to see that whatever exits in our difficult circumstances, we accept and believe that it is God's hand. The Lord can never do any wrong.

Second, another great hindrance in breaking the outer man is self-love. We must ask God to take away the heart of self-love. As He deals with us in response to our prayer, we should worship and say, "O Lord, if this be Your hand, let me accept it from my heart." Let us remember that the one reason for all misunderstandings, all fretfulness, all disappointments, is that we secretly love ourselves. Hence, we plan a way whereby we can rescue ourselves. Many times problems arise due to our seeking a way of escape—an escape from the working of the cross.

He who has ascended the cross and refuses to drink the vinegar mingled with gall is the one who knows the Lord. Many go up to the cross rather reluctantly, still thinking of drinking vinegar mingled with gall to alleviate their pain. All who say— *"The cup which the Father has given me, shall I not drink it?"*—will not drink the cup of vinegar mingled with gall. They can only drink of one cup, not two! Only such ones as these are the ones without self-love. Self-love is a basic difficulty with most believers. May the Lord speak to us today that we may be able to pray: "O my God, I have seen that all things come from You. All my hardships these past five, ten, or twenty years, are of

19

You. You have so worked to attain Your purpose, which is none other than You living Your life through me. But I have been foolish. I failed to see this. I did many things to defend myself, thus delaying Your time. Today, I see Your hand in all of my situations. I am willing to offer myself to You. Once again, I place myself in Your hands."

Expect to See Wounds

No life manifests more beauty than the one who is broken! Stubbornness and self-love have given way to beauty in the one who has been broken by God. For example, consider Jacob in the Old Testament. We see how even in his mother's womb he struggled with his brother. He was subtle, tricky, and manipulative. But his life was full of sorrows and grief. As a youth, he fled from home. For twenty years, he was cheated by Laban. The wife of his heart's love—Rachel—died prematurely. The son of his love—Joseph—was sold into slavery. Years later, another one of his dearly loved sons, Benjamin, was detained in Egypt. Repeatedly, he was dealt with by God, meeting misfortune after misfortune. He was stricken by God once, twice, and thrice. Indeed, his whole history is said to be a history of being stricken by God. Finally, after many recurring dealings, the man Jacob was transformed. In his last few years, he was quite transparent. How dignified was his answer to Pharaoh! How beautiful was his end when he worshiped God leaning on his staff! How clear were his blessings to his descendants! After reading the last page of his history, we want to bow our heads and worship God. Here is one who is matured, who knows God so experientially. Several decades of dealings have resulted in the breaking of Jacob's outward man. In his old age, his life of brokenness is a picture of beauty.

Each one of us has as much of the same "Jacob-nature" in us. Our only hope is that the Lord may blaze a way out of us, breaking our outward man—breaking it to such a degree that the inward man may come out and be seen. This is precious! This is the way for those who serve the Lord. Only by this process can we serve the Lord, and only by this procedure can we lead men to the Lord. All else is limited in its value. Doctrinal and theological knowledge does not have that much usefulness. What is the use of mere mental knowledge of the Bible if the outward man remains unbroken? Only the person through whom God can come forth is useful.

After our outward man has been stricken, dealt with, and led through various trials, we have wounds upon us, thus allowing the spirit to emerge. We are afraid to meet some brothers and sisters whose whole being remains intact. They never had been dealt with and therefore exhibit no change. May God have mercy upon us to clearly show us this way. That this is the only way, only He can reveal. May He also show us the important purpose of all His dealings within these past few years—say ten, fifteen, or twenty years—it is the breaking of the outward man for the release of our inward man, our spirit. Therefore, let no one despise the Lord's dealings. May He truly reveal to us what is meant by the breaking of the outward man. Should the outward man remain whole, everything would then be merely in our mind and remain utterly useless. Let us expect the Lord to deal with our outward man thoroughly for the release of our spirit.

2

Before and After Brokenness

THE BREAKING of the outward man is the basic experience of all who serve God. This must be accomplished before He can use us effectively. When one is working for God, two possibilities may arise. The **first** is the unbrokenness of self, forming a hard shell around the spirit. It is possible, when the outward man remains unbroken, that his spirit may be inert and unable to function. This means that if he is a clever intellectual person, his mind governs his work. Or, if he is a generous charitable person, his emotions control his actions. His work may appear successful, but it cannot bring people to God. The **second** is the mixture of his spirit with his unbroken self. His spirit may come forth clad with strong thoughts or emotions of self. The result is that both his spirit and soul are mixed and impure. Consequently, his work will bring men into a mixed and impure experience. These two conditions illustrate how unbroken self will weaken our service to God.

If we desire to work effectively, we must realize that basically *"it is the Spirit which gives life"* (Jn. 6:63; 2 Cor. 3:6). Sooner or later—if not on the first day of our salvation, then perhaps ten years later—we must recognize this fact. Many have to be brought to their wit's end in order to see the emptiness of their labor, and to recognize the uselessness of their many thoughts and varied emotions. Regardless how many people can be attracted by your thoughts or emotions, the results will still come to nothing. Eventually, we must confess: *"It is the Spirit which gives life."* The Spirit alone makes people live. Your best thought or your best emotion cannot make people live. Man is brought into life only by the Spirit. Many who serve the Lord will eventually come to see this fact only after passing through much sorrow and many failures. Then finally, the Lord's Word becomes meaningful to them: *"That which gives life is the Spirit."* When the **spirit** is released, then sinners are born anew and saints are edified. When life is communicated through the channel of the spirit, people who receive it are born anew. When life is supplied through the spirit to believers, they are edified. Without the Spirit, there can be no new birth and no edification.

One rather remarkable thing is that God does not often distinguish between His Spirit and our spirit. There are many places in the Bible where it is impossible to determine whether the word *"spirit"* indicates our human spirit or God's Spirit. Bible translators, from Luther down to present day scholars who have labored on their English versions, have been unable to decide if the word *"spirit,"* as it is often used in several places of the New Testament, refers to the human spirit or to the Spirit of God.

For example, of the whole Bible Romans eight may very well be the chapter where the word *"spirit"* is used most frequently. Who can discern how many times the word *"spirit"* in this chapter refers to the human spirit and how many times to God's Spirit? In various English versions, the Greek word **pneuma** is translated *"spirit."* But this word is sometimes capitalized, and at other times it is written without any capitalization. It is evident that these versions do not consistently agree with each other. Moreover, not one scholar's opinion is final, because it is simply impossible to distinguish. When we received our new spirit through regeneration, simultaneously, we also received God's Spirit. The moment our human spirit is raised from the state of death, we receive the Holy Spirit. We often say that the Holy Spirit dwells **in** our spirit, but we find it perplexing to discern which is the Holy Spirit and which is our own human spirit. The Holy Spirit and our spirit have become so joined together. While each is uniquely separate, they nevertheless are not so easily distinguishable.

Thus, the release of the spirit is the release of both the human spirit as well as the Divine Spirit, Who resides in the spirit of man. Since the Holy Spirit and our spirit are joined as one (I Cor. 6.17), many times they are distinguishable in name only, not in fact. And since the release of one means the release of both, the Holy Spirit is touched when our spirit is touched. Thank God that inasmuch as you allow people to contact your spirit, you allow them to contact God. Your spirit has brought the Holy Spirit to man.

When the Holy Spirit is working, He needs to be carried by the human spirit. For example, the electricity in an electric bulb does not travel like lightning. Its current must be conducted through electric wires. If you want to use electricity, you need electric wires to bring it to you. In like manner, the Spirit of God employs the human spirit as His carrier, and through it He is brought to man.

Everyone who has received grace through redemption has the Holy Spirit dwelling in his spirit. However, whether he can be used by the Lord depends not on his spirit, but rather on his outward man. The obstacle with many people is that their outward man has not been broken. There is no evidence of the sufferings which leave their wounds or scars upon their soulish life. So God's Spirit is imprisoned within man's spirit. Consequently, the life-giving Spirit (1 Cor. 15:45) is not able to break out of the shell constituted with the outward man.

25

Sometimes our outward man is active, while the inward man remains inactive. The outward man has gone forth, but the inward man lags behind.

Some Practical Problems

Let us review some practical problems! Take preaching, for instance. How often we can be earnestly preaching—giving a well prepared and well thought-out message—but inwardly we feel as cold as ice. We long to stir others, yet we ourselves are unmoved. There is a lack of harmony between the outward and the inward man. The outward man is sweating from heat, but the inward man is shivering from coldness. We can tell others how great the love of the Lord is, yet we are personally untouched by it. We can tell others how tragic is the suffering of the cross, yet upon returning to our room we can clown around. What can we do about this? Minds may labor and emotions may be energized. Yet all throughout the endeavor, one has the feeling that the inward man is merely an observer—not a participant—of the outward man's performance. Here again we see that the outward and the inward man are not compatibly one.

Consider the opposite situation. The inward man is devoured by zeal. He wants to shout, but he does not find utterance. After speaking for a long time, the speaker still seems to be talking in circles. The more he is burdened **within**, the colder he becomes **without**. He longs to speak, but he cannot express himself. When he meets a sinner and his inward man feels like weeping, he cannot shed a tear. There is a sense of urgency within him, yet when he ascends the pulpit and tries to proclaim it, he finds himself lost in a maze of words. Such a situation is most trying. The root cause is the same—the outer shell still clings to him. The outward does not obey the dictates of the inward—**inwardly** crying, but **outwardly** unmoved. **Inwardly** suffering, but **outwardly** untouched. Full of thoughts **within**, but the mind **without** draws an apparent blank. In other words, his inner spirit has yet to find a way to pierce through his outer shell.

Thus, the breaking of the outward man is the very first lesson for everyone who wants to learn to serve God. He who is truly used by God is one whose outward thought and outward emotion do not act independently of his spirit. If we have not learned this lesson, we shall find that our effectiveness is greatly impaired. May God bring us to the place and show us the pathway where the outward man is completely broken.

When such a condition of brokenness prevails, there will be an end to the dichotomy of outward activity with inward inertness. An end to inward crying with outward composure. An end to an abundance of inner thoughts for which there is no utterance. A broken man will not be poor in thought. He does not need to use twenty sentences to express what can be said in two. His thoughts will assist him instead of hindering his spirit.

Likewise, our emotions can also be a very hard shell. Many who desire to be happy cannot express joy. Or, they may wish to weep, but cannot. If the Lord has stricken our outward man—either through the discipline or by the enlightenment of the Holy Spirit—we are able to express joy or sorrow according to the dictates of the inner man.

The release of our spirit makes it possible for us to abide increasingly in God. We can also touch the spirit of revelation in the Bible. Without effort, our spirit can receive divine illumination. When we are witnessing or preaching, we can send forth God's Word through our spirit. Furthermore, we can use our released spirit to spontaneously contact the spirit in others. Whenever someone speaks in our presence, we can intuitively identify him—evaluate his character, his attitudes, the state of his Christian life, and his current spiritual needs. Our spirit can touch his spirit. And what is wonderful is that others can easily contact our spirit. With some, we meet merely their thoughts, or their emotions, or their will. Consequently, after conversing with them for hours, we still have not met the spirit

27

of their real person, even though we may both be Christians. The outer shell is simply too thick for others to penetrate the condition of their inner man. However, by the breaking of the outward man, the spirit begins to flow freely and is ever open transparently to others.

Launching Out and Retreating

Once the outward man is broken, man's spirit abides spontaneously and constantly in the presence of God. Two years after a certain brother trusted in the Lord, he read THE PRACTICE OF THE PRESENCE OF GOD by Brother Lawrence. After reading it, he felt grieved at his failure to abide unceasingly in the presence of God like Brother Lawrence. At the time he had hourly appointments to pray with someone. Why? Well, since the Bible says, *"Pray without ceasing,"* they thought it meant "Pray every hour." Every time they heard the clock strike at the top of the hour, they would pray.

They exerted their utmost effort to retreat into God, because they felt they could not maintain themselves continuously in the presence of God. It was as if they had slipped away while working, and thus needed to retreat quickly back to God. Or they had projected themselves out while studying, and now they must withdraw swiftly back to God. Otherwise, they would find themselves away from God for the whole day. They prayed often, spending whole days in prayer on the Lord's Day and half-days on Saturday. They continued this for two or three years.

Nevertheless, the trouble remained. When withdrawing to pray, they enjoyed God's presence. But when going about their daily responsibilities, they lost it. Of course, this is not only their problem alone; it is also the experience of many Christians. It indicates we are trying to maintain God's presence by the effort of our memory. The sense of His presence fluctuates according to our memory. When we remember, there is the consciousness of His presence. Otherwise, there is none. This is sheer folly when we discover that God's

28

presence is in the spirit of our inner man, and **not** in the memory of our outer man.

To solve this problem, we must first settle the question of the breaking the outward man. Since neither our emotions nor our thoughts has the same nature as God, it cannot be joined to Him. The Gospel of John shows us something about the nature of God—*"God is Spirit"* (4:24). And our human spirit alone is of the same nature as God—*"and they that worship Him must worship Him in spirit."* Therefore, our human spirit can be synchronized with His Divine Spirit. If we try to get the presence of God by directing our thoughts on God, then His presence will appear lost when we lose our concentration on God.

Likewise, if we seek to use our emotions to summon the presence of God, then His presence seems to disappear as soon as we start relaxing. Sometimes when we are happy, we take this to mean we have the presence of God. So when our happiness ceases, his presence flees! Or we may assume that His presence is with us if we mourn and weep. Alas, some of us haven't shed a tear throughout our entire life! However, whatever tears we can conjure up, soon our tears will dry up, and then God's presence seems to disappear again.

Both our thoughts and our emotions are endeavors derived from the human energies of the outward man. All such activity must eventually come to an end. If we try to maintain God's presence with that sort of activity, then His presence ends when such activity ceases. However, God's presence requires the sameness of nature. Only the inward man is of the same nature as God. Through his spirit alone can His presence be manifested. The constant activities of the outward man will only disturb the inward man. Thus, the outward man is not a helper but a disturber. When the outward man is broken, the inward man enjoys continual rest in God.

The human spirit God has given to us enables us to respond to Him. However, the outward man is ever responding to his endeavors without; hence, depriving us of the presence of God. We cannot destroy all the external distractions which exist without, but we can cooperate with God to break down the outward man. We cannot put a stop to all the things without. Millions and billions of things in the world are utterly beyond our control. Whenever anything happens, our outward man will respond; consequently, we are not able to enjoy God's presence in peace. We conclude, therefore, that experiencing the presence of God is contingent upon the breaking of our outward man.

If, through the mercy of God, our outward man has been broken, we may be characterized by the following: Yesterday we were full of curiosity, but today it is impossible to be curious. Formerly our emotions could be easily aroused—either stirring our love, the most delicate emotion, or provoking our temper, the crudest emotion. But now, regardless of how many things crowd upon us, our inward man remains unmoved, the presence of God is unchanged, and our inner peace unruffled.

It now should become evident to us that the breaking of the outward man is the basis for enjoying God's abiding presence. Remember when Brother Lawrence was engaged in kitchen work. People were clamoring around him for things they wanted. Although there were the constant clatter of dishes and utensils, his inward man was not disturbed. He could sense God's presence in the hustle and bustle of a kitchen as much as in quiet prayer. Why? He was impervious to external noises. He had learned the secret of communing **in his spirit** while ignoring his soul life.

Some feel that to have God's presence, their environment must be free of such distractions as the clatter of dishes. The farther away they are from mankind, the better they will be able to sense the presence of God. What a mistake! The trouble lies not in those dishes, nor in other people, but in themselves. God is not going to deliver us from "the dishes"! But He will deliver us from our responses! In spite of how noisy it is on the outside, what is inside of us never needs to respond. Since the Lord has broken our outward man, we simply react calmly as though we had not heard. Praise the Lord, we may possess a very keen sense of hearing, but due to the work of grace in our lives, we are not at all influenced by the pressures surrounding our outward man. We can be before God in the midst of utter distractions just as much as when we are praying somewhere alone. Once the outward man is broken, he no longer needs to retreat Godward, for he is always in the presence of God. Not so with the one whose outward man is still intact. After running an errand, he feels the compelling need to return, for he assumes he has moved away from God. Even while doing the work of the Lord, he presumes that he has slipped away from the One he serves. So it seems the best thing for him to do is not to do anything or make any movements. Nevertheless, those who know God do not need to return, for they have never been away. They enjoy the presence of God when they set aside a day for prayer, and they enjoy the same presence to the same degree when they are busily engaged in the menial tasks of life.

Perhaps it is our common experience, when in drawing near to God, we sense His presence. But if we are engaged in some activity, in spite of our vigilance, we feel that somehow we have drifted away. Suppose, for example, we are preaching the gospel or trying to edify people. After a while, we feel like kneeling down to pray. But we have a sense that we must first retreat into God. Somehow our conversation with people has led us a little away from God. So through prayer, we must first draw closer to Him. We have lost God's presence. So now we must have it restored to us.

Or, we may be occupied with some menial task, such as scrubbing the floors. Upon completing our task, we decide to pray. Once again we feel we have taken a long trip away from God and must now return. What is the answer to these problems? It must be emphasized that the breaking of the outward man makes such returns unnecessary. We sense the presence of God in our conversation as much as in kneeling in prayer. Performing our menial tasks does not draw us away from God; hence, it is unnecessary to return.

Now let us consider an extreme case in order to illustrate this better. Anger is one of the most crude of human feelings. But the Bible does not prohibit us to be angry, because some types of anger are not related to sin. The Bible says, *"Be angry but sin not"* (Eph. 4:26). Nonetheless, anger of any kind is so strong that it nearly always borders on sin. We do not find a verse in God's Word charging us to "love but sin not" or "be meek but sin not." Why? Because love and meekness are far removed from sin. But anger is close to the vicinity of sin.

Perhaps a certain brother has committed a serious blunder. He severely needs to be reprimanded. This is not an easy matter. Instead, we would exercise our feelings of mercy rather than bring our feelings of anger into play, because the latter can fall into something detrimental with the least of carelessness. Hence, it is not easy to be properly angry according to the will of God. But when one knows the breaking of his outward man, he can deal severely with another brother without his own spirit being disturbed or God's presence interrupted. He continues abiding in God just as much when he is dealing with others as he does when he is praying. Therefore, after he has taken his brother to task, he can pray without any exercise of retreating back to God. Of course, we acknowledge that this is rather difficult. But when the outward man is broken, it can well be the case.

Dividing the Outward from the Inward

When the outward man is broken, things outside will be kept outside, and the inward man will live continuously before God. That is the first problem which we have solved. Now the second problem with many is that their outward man and their inward man are so intertwined together that what influences the outward also impacts the inward. Through the merciful workings of God, the outward man must be separated from the inward man. Therefore, what affects the outward will not be able to reach the inward. While the outward man may become engaged in conversation, the inward man fellowships with God. The outward may be burdened with listening to the clatter of dishes, yet the inward abides in God. One is able to carry on activities or to contact the world with the outer man; nevertheless, the inner man remains unaffected because he still lives before God.

Consider an example or two. A certain brother is working on the road. If his outer and inner man have been divided, the latter will not be disturbed by outside things. He can labor in his outward man, while at the same time he is inwardly worshiping God.

Or consider a parent. His outward man may be laughing and playing with his little child. Suddenly, a certain spiritual need arises. He can at once meet the situation with his inward man, for he has never been absent from the presence of God. So it is important for us to realize that the dividing of the outward and inward man has a most decisive effect upon one's daily work and life. Only in thus separating the two can one be able to labor without distraction.

We may describe believers as either a "single" person or a "dual" person. With some, their inner and outer man are one—hence, a single person. But with others, the two are separate—thus, a dual person. As long as one is a "single" person, with the inner and outer mixed as one, he must summon his whole being either into his work at one time or into his prayer at another. When working, he leaves God behind. Later, when praying, he must turn away from his work. Because his outward man has not been broken, he is forced to launch out and retreat.

The "dual" person, on the other hand, is able to work with his outward man, while remaining constantly before God with his inward man. Whenever the need arises, his inward man can break forth and manifest itself before others. He enjoys the unbroken presence of God.

Let us ask ourselves: Am I a "single" person or a "dual" person? Having the outward man divided from the inward does make all the difference. If through the mercy of God you have experienced this dividing, then while you are working or are outwardly active, you know there is a man within you who remains calm. Although the outward man is engaged in external things, these will not penetrate into the inward man.

Here is the wondrous secret! The presence of God is known through the dividing of these two. Brother Lawrence seemed to be busily occupied with kitchen work; yet within him was another man standing before God and enjoying undisturbed communion with Him. Such an inner separation will keep our reactions free from the defilement of flesh and blood.

In conclusion, let us remember that the ability to use our spirit depends upon the two-fold work of God: The breaking of the outward man. And the dividing of spirit and soul—the separating of our inward man from the outward. Only after God has carried out both of these processes in our lives are we able to exercise our spirit. First, the outward man is broken through **the discipline of the Holy Spirit.** Second, the outward is divided from the inward man by **the revelation of the Holy Spirit** (Heb. 4:12). More about both of these matters will be covered in later chapters.

3

Recognizing
"The Thing In Hand"

LET ME FIRST explain our topic. Suppose a father urges his son to do something for him. The son answers, "Right now I have something in my hand. As soon as I finish this, I will come and do it for you." "**The thing in hand**" is the thing which the son is doing prior to his father's summons. Immediately, we recognize the preoccupation of those "things in our hands" will hinder us in our walk with God and delay His work. It might be anything—a good, important, or seemingly necessary thing—which preoccupies us and diverts our attention. As long as the outward man remains unbroken, we shall most likely find our hands full of things. Our outward man has its own religious activities, recreational diversions, business concerns, and other side-interests. So when the Spirit of God moves in our spirit, our outward man cannot answer God's call. Thus, it is the "thing in hand" which blocks the way to spiritual usefulness.

The Limited Strength of the Outward Man

Our human strength is limited. If a brother can only carry fifty pounds, he simply cannot carry an additional ten. He is a person with limited strength, unable to do unlimited work. The fifty pounds he is already carrying is "the thing in hand." Just as the physical strength of our outermost man—our physical body— is limited, so it is with the strength of our outward man—our soul. Many, not realizing this principle, carelessly deplete the strength of their outward man. If, for example, one lavished all his love upon his parents, he has no strength left for loving his brothers, not to mention others. In exhausting his strength, there is nothing left to spend for others.

So it is with our mental strength. If one's attention is focused on one matter, and he exhausts all his time in thinking about it, he will have no strength to think about other matters. In His Word, God has explained our problem: *"The law of the Spirit of life in Christ Jesus has set me free from the law of sin and of death"* (Rom. 8:2). But why is this law of the Spirit of life ineffectual in certain people? Again, we read: *"The righteous requirement of the law should be fulfilled in us who walk ... according to Spirit"* (Rom. 8:4). In other words, the law of the Spirit of life works effectively only for those who are spiritual—those who mind the things of the Spirit. Who are they? They are the ones who do not mind the things of the flesh. The word *"mind"* in verse 5 can also be translated *"to be intent upon, to be attentive to."*

For instance, a mother, who is going out, leaves her baby in the care of a friend. To take care of the baby means to give your attention to him. When you are entrusted with the care of a baby, you dare not be preoccupied with other things. This illustrates how those whose attention is **not** preoccupied by carnal things can be attentive to spiritual things. Those who have the intent and purpose to pursue spiritual things can come under the control of the Holy Spirit. Our mental strength is limited. If we exhaust it on the things of the flesh, we shall find ourselves mentally inadequate for the things of the Spirit.

We realize, then, that just as our physical strength is limited, so it is with the mental strength of our outward man. As long as we have "things in hand," we cannot serve God. According to the number of things in our hand, strength for serving God either decreases or increases. Hence, "the thing in hand" becomes indeed a hindrance, and this is not inconsequential.

Again, one may have many things in hand emotionally—such as, various likes and dislikes, personal inclinations, or wishful expectations. All these things pull at him like a magnetic attraction. When God asks a person for his affections, having so many things in hand, he cannot respond. Why? Because he has already used up all his emotional strength for other things. His hands, being too full of other things, do not have enough space for another thing. If he is exhausted after expending two days worth of emotional resources, it will be that long again before he can feel adequately restored and refreshed. When emotions are wasted on lesser things, it is not accessible for God's use.

There are those moreover who manifest an iron will—those with strong personalities whose volitional powers seem unlimited. Yet, strange as it might seem, he seems unable to make up his mind in the things of God. How often the strongest person, in making his decisions before God, will waver! Why is this?

Before we answer this, let us consider another category of persons who are full of ideas. Although he never seems to be at a loss for words, having an opinion for everything, yet when it comes to discerning the will of God in spiritual things, he is utterly void of light. Why is this so?

While the outward man is so weighted down with the things in hand and thereby becomes so exhausted, there is little strength left for any spiritual exercise. It is needful, then, to see the limited strength of the outer man. Even though this outer man is broken, there must still be wisdom in using his limited strength. How necessary it is, then, to have "**empty hands**"!

The Spirit's Use of a Broken Outward Man

In His dealings with man, God's Spirit never circumvents a man's spirit. Neither can a man's spirit circumvent the outer man. This is a most important principle to grasp. As the Holy Spirit does not bypass man's spirit in His work with man, so no more does our spirit bypass our outward man in our work with others. In order to touch other lives, our spirit must pass through our outward man. Hence, when our strength is consumed by the fixations of many things at hand, God cannot do His work through us. This means the outlet of our outward man for both the human spirit and the Holy Spirit is totally unavailable. The inward man cannot come forth, because he is blocked by an exhausted outward man. That is why we have repeatedly suggested that this outward man must be broken.

"The thing in hand" stands in the way, preventing God from doing His work. This "thing" is something not connected to God. This "thing" is so promoted that His will, His power, or His decision can not be carried out. It is something not under the hand of God, but rather something under the independent hand of an unbroken self.

Before your outward man is broken, you are occupied with your own things. You walk in your own way. You love your own people. If God wants to use your love in loving the brethren, He must first break your outward man. This love of yours is thereby enlarged. The inward man must love, but he has to love through the outward man. If the outward man is consumed with "the thing in hand," the inward man is deprived of a proper channel for loving.

Again, when the inward man needs to use his will, he finds it acting independently, already strongly engaged by the thing already existing in his hand. To break our will, God must strike us with a

38

heavy blow until we prostrate ourselves in the dust and say, "Lord, I dare not think, I dare not ask, I dare not decide on my own. In each and every thing I need Thee." In being thus stricken, we learn that our will is not to act independently of God. Only then is our will ready to be used by the inward man.

Without the cooperation of the outward man, the inward man is most handicapped. Suppose a brother is going to preach the Word. He has a burden in his spirit. However, if he fails to find corresponding thoughts, he cannot release his burden, and it will soon fade away. Even though the burden may permeate his whole spirit, all is futile if his mind is unable to communicate it.

We cannot bring men to salvation merely with the burden in our spirit. It must also be expressed through our mind. The burden within must be coordinated with the mind and mouth without. Without utterance, it is impossible to make known to others the Word of God. Man's words are not God's Word, but the latter must be communicated by the former. When man has God's words, God can speak. When he does not, God cannot speak. The trouble today is this: While our inward man is available to God, being able to receive God's burden, yet our outward man is driven by such myriads of confusing thoughts from morning till night that our spirit is blocked, failing to find an outlet.

Thus it is that God must crush our outward man. He breaks our will by taking away the things held in our will's "hand" so that it cannot act independently. It is not that we are mindless, having no mind. But the point is that we should not think after the flesh and not think according to our wandering imaginations. It is not that we are devoid of emotions, but that all our emotions, we emphatically declare, are under the control and restraint of the inward man. Brokenness gives the inner man a pliable and usable will, mind, and emotions. God wants our spirit to use our outward man for deciding, for thinking, and for loving. It is not His thought to annihilate our outward man. But we must receive this basic experience of being

39

broken if we aspire to be effectual in the service of God toward others.

Until this happens, the inward and the outward man are at odds with each other, because the outer is acting independently of the inner. When we are broken, the outward man is under the control of the inward, which has an unifying effect in our personality. As a result, the shattered outward man becomes a channel of life for the inward man.

Now by contrast, it must be recognized that a unified personality may often characterize an unsaved person. In this case, the inward man is under the control of his outward man. Although the human spirit exists, it is so beaten down by the outward man that it can at best only arouse a few moral protests from its conscience. Hence, such an inward man is utterly dominated by the outward man.

However, after one is saved, it is God's intention that he should experience a reversal of this order. Just as much as his outward man controlled the inward before he was saved, so now his inward man should hold absolute sway over the outward after he is saved.

We can use bicycling as an illustration. On flat ground, we can control the bicycle by peddling its wheels on the road. Similarly, when our inward man is strong, we can "pedal" and control the bicycle along the way. We may decide to stop, continue, or determine how fast to go. However, in the case of a bicycle going down a very steep hill, the wheels rotate without any pedaling at all. Suddenly, we become powerless, as the road before us seems to hurriedly thrust us along, plunging us out of control. Likewise, if our outward man is hard and unbroken, we will be like a bicycle coasting out of control down a steep incline. Should the Lord be gracious to us and level out the "steep slopes" of our outward man by means of breaking—so that we can no longer give dogmatic opinions impulsively and make self-centered decisions independently—we shall be as those who are able to properly use their spirit.

A Broken Person Not Taught

No one is equipped to do God's work simply because he has learned some teachings. The basic question is still this: What kind of man is he? Can one who is unbroken, but whose teachings are right, supply the need of the church? So the basic lesson we must learn is to be transformed into a vessel prepared for the Master's use. This can only be done by the breaking process of the outward man.

God is at work in our lives unceasingly. The many years of sufferings, trials, and hindrances depict the hand of God, Who is daily seeking to carry on His work of breaking us. Do you not see what God is doing in the endless round of difficulties in your life? If not, you should ask Him, "O God, open my eyes that I may see Thy hand."

How often the eyes of an Balaam's burro are sharper than those of a self-styled prophet. Although the burro had already seen the Angel of the Lord, his master had not. The burro recognized the forbidding hand of God, but the self-styled prophet did not. We should be aware that brokenness is God's way for our lives. How sad that some still imagine that if they could only absorb more doctrinal teachings, accumulate more preaching materials, and assimilate more Biblical expositions, they would be profitable to God. This is absolutely wrong. God's hand is upon you to break you. Not according to your will, but His! Not according to your thoughts, but His! Not according to your decision, but His! Our difficulty is that while God withstands us, we blame others. We react like that prophet who, blind to God's hand, blamed the burro for refusing to budge.

All that comes to us is ordered by God. To us as Christians, **nothing** is accidental. We should ask God to open our eyes to see that it is He Who is striking us by all things and in all areas of our life. One day, when we are enabled by His grace to accept the ordering of God in our environment, our spirit will be released and ready to function.

One Law Unaffected By Prayer

There is an immutable law of God's working in our lives: His one specific purpose is to break us and to release our spirit for its free exercise. We must understand that none of our praying, pleading, or promising will affect His purpose or change His mind. It is according to this unchangeable law of purpose that He will accomplish both the brokenness and the release in all of us. All of our praying will not alter His law. For instance, if you deliberately thrust your hand into the fire, will prayer prevent your hand from scorching pain? If you do not wish to be burnt by fire and yet you deliberately thrust your hand into it anyway, do not then think that prayer will save you from consequences. It will not. In like manner, let us see that God's dealing with us is deliberately according to His law. In order for life to come forth, the inward man must pass through the outward. Until our outward man is shattered, the inward simply cannot be released and come forth. Do not try to oppose and overturn this law and its effects by praying for blessings. Such prayers are in vain. Praying can never change God's law.

We must settle this once and for all. The way of spiritual work counts on God's Spirit passing through our inner man. This is the only way God has ordained. To one whose outer man is unbroken, the gospel is blocked and cannot flow out. Let us bow low before God. To obey God's law is far better than saying many prayers. It is much better to stop praying and confess: "God, I prostrate myself before Thee." Yes, how often our prayers for blessings can actually raise up barriers. We long for God's blessing, but instead we seem to find God's mercy in our crushing experiences. If only we would seek for enlightenment, learn to submit ourselves to His hand, and obey His law, we would find that the outcome is the very blessing we deeply long for.

4

How To Know Man

T O KNOW MAN is vital in the Lord's work. When someone comes to us, we must discern his spiritual condition, including what he was and what he has now become. We must determine whether he has said what is really in his heart and how much he has left unsaid. Further, we should perceive his obvious characteristics— whether he is hardhearted or humble, and whether his humility is true or false. Our effectiveness in service is closely related to our discernment of man's spiritual condition. If God's Spirit enables us through our spirit to know the condition of the person before us, we can then impart the appropriate word.

In the Gospels we find that whenever men came to our Lord, He always had the right word. This is marvelous! The Lord did not talk to the Samaritan woman about the new birth, nor did he tell

Nicodemus of living water. The truth of the new birth was for Nicodemus, while the truth of the living water was for the Samaritan woman. How appropriate! Moreover, those who had not followed Him were invited to come. But those who desired to follow Him were invited to bear the cross. Also, to the one who volunteered, He spoke of counting the cost. While to the one who lingered, He said, "Let the dead bury their dead." His words were always most appropriate, for **the Lord knew all men.** Our Lord knew whether they came as earnest seekers or merely to spy on Him. And what He said to them was always right on target. May our Lord be merciful to us so that from Him we also may learn how to know man in order to be more effective in helping people.

Without much acquired knowledge, a brother can only handle souls by his own limited understanding. One day, if he acquires a special feeling, he will speak it to everybody. If he has a favorite subject, he speaks on it everywhere. How can his work be effective? No physician will use the same prescription for all his patients. Regrettably, some who serve God have only one prescription for everyone. Although they cannot diagnose people's sicknesses, they try to cure them anyway. In spite of their ignorance of man's complexities and their lack of insight into man's spiritual condition, they nonetheless are too eager and zealous to treat every ailment. How foolish it is to have only one spiritual prescription to meet every kind of spiritual disorder!

Perhaps you imagined that the naive can never discern but that the clever can? No, in the Lord's work both the clever and the naive are equally excluded. You cannot use your independent mind or personal feelings to discern people. However keen your mind, it alone can never penetrate the depths of man and reveal his condition.

It is important for each worker to first discern what is the individual's real need before God. Frequently, you cannot depend on what he says. Although he may have correctly insisted that he has a "headache," it may be only a symptom of a deeper condition whose

44

roots are to be found elsewhere. Just because he feels warm does not necessarily mean he has a "high fever." He is likely to tell you many things which have no bearing on his case. A "sick person" seldom understands his own health problems; so he needs someone else to diagnose it and prescribe the right cure. You may want him to tell you something about his need, but he is prone to be mistaken. Only a trained diagnostician, skilled in recognizing spiritual ailments, can discern the "patient's" real need. In every diagnosis, you must insist on exactness and accuracy. One who is merely subjective is sure to inflict people with imaginative illnesses, relentlessly imposing his opinions upon them as to what ails them.

Sometimes we may discover that a particular problem is beyond our ability to help. Do not be so foolish to assume you can cope with every situation and help solve all problems. For those whom you can help, you should spend yourself and be spent. But when you cannot be of help, you should humbly tell the Lord, "This is beyond my ability; I cannot discern his disease. I haven't learned enough about it yet. Oh, Lord, be merciful!" We should never think we can handle everyone's spiritual need and try to monopolize the work. Here is our chance to see the supply from the different members of the Body. If you feel a certain brother or sister can handle the emergency, seek him out and honestly say, "This is beyond my measure. Perhaps this is within your expertise." By working together in the Body, we learn how to act relatedly, and not independently.

We must emphasize it again: Every worker must learn before the Lord **how to know man**. How many lives were spoiled after passing through the hands of zealous brothers who have not learned this. They vainly and impulsively give their subjective opinions to meet simple objective needs! People are not necessarily afflicted with the ailments that we imagine. Our responsibility is to discern their true spiritual condition. If we ourselves had not first experienced and understood our own spiritual problems, how can we hope to help the rest of God's children?

45

We Ourselves His Instrumentalities

In diagnosing a case, a medical doctor has access to many of his medical instruments. This is not so with us. We have no thermometer, no x-ray, nor any other such devices to help us discern a man's spiritual condition. How, then, do we discern whether a brother is spiritually ill? How do we determine the nature of his trouble? It is wonderful that God has designed **us**—yes, **us!**—to be like "thermometers" to read another person's spiritual temperature. By His working in our own lives, He would equip us to discern what "ails" a person. As the Lord's spiritual "doctors," we must have a thorough inward preparation. We must be deeply conscious of the weight of our responsibility.

Suppose the thermometer had never been invented. The doctor, like in previous generations, would have to determine whether his patient had a fever by the mere touch of his hand. His hand would serve as the thermometer. How sensitive and accurate the touch of his hand would need to be! In spiritual work, this is exactly the case.

We ourselves are God's thermometers and God's instruments. We must undergo thorough training and strict discipline, because whatever is left untouched in us will be left untouched in others. Moreover, we cannot help others in areas which we ourselves have not learned the lessons before God. The more thorough our training, the greater will be our usefulness in God's work. Likewise, the more we spare ourselves—our pride, our narrow opinions, yes, even our feelings of happiness—the less will be our usefulness. If we have spared these things in ourselves, we cannot touch them in others. A proud person cannot deal with the pride of another. A hypocrite cannot touch the hypocrisy in another. Neither can one who lives a loose life have a helpful impact on one who suffers the same difficulty. How well we know that if something persists in our nature, we will not be able to condemn that particular sin in others. In fact, we will hardly recognize it in others. A doctor in the physical realm may cure others without curing himself, but this can hardly be true in the spiritual realm. The worker himself is first a patient. He must first himself be healed before he can heal others. What he has not seen cannot be shown to others. He cannot lead others where he has not trodden. He cannot teach others what he himself has not learned.

We must see that we are **ourselves** the instruments God prepares for knowing man. Hence, our persona must be dependable and qualified in order to give an accurate diagnosis. So that our feelings may be reliable, we need to pray, "O Lord, do not let me go untouched, unbroken, and unprepared." We must allow God to work in us to such an extent undreamed of before, so that we may become a more prepared and useable vessel. A doctor would never use a defective thermometer. How much more deficient and ill-advised it is for us to use our untouched thoughts, emotions, opinions, and ways to touch the spiritual conditions of others. To impulsively do one thing and suddenly do another indicates that we are yet unstable. How can we be useable when we are so undependable? Our efforts will simply be in vain. Consequently, we must pass through God's dealings.

Repeatedly, we must face this question: Are we really conscious of the seriousness of our responsibility? God's Spirit does **not** always work directly on people. But mostly, He does His work **through** man. People's needs are met, on the one hand, by the discipline of the Holy Spirit. In other words, He sovereignly orders their environment. And on the other hand, they are dealt with by the ministry of the Word. Without the supply of the ministry of the Word, the spiritual problem of the saints cannot be solved. What responsibility has fallen upon His workers! It is most solemn and imperative. A person's usefulness determines the breadth and depth of supply that can be offered to the church.

Suppose it is characteristic of a certain illness to reach a temperature of, say, 103° F. Unless you know the exact temperature, your diagnosis cannot be certain. You cannot simply guess it by touching the patient with your hand that his fever is somewhat about103 °. Even in the spiritual realm, it would be too risky for us to try to help others when our feelings and opinions are mistaken and our spiritual understanding is inadequate. Only when we are tested and tried, until we become accurate and trustworthy, can the Spirit of God be released through us.

The starting point of a spiritual work is marked by the many readjustments made before God. A thermometer is manufactured according to certain standards and is carefully examined to meet rigid specifications. If, then, we are the Lord's thermometer, how strict must be the discipline to bring us up to God's standard of accuracy! In God's work, we are both "doctors" and "medical instruments." How important it is that we pass His test!

Our Key Perception for Knowing Man

Knowing a patient's condition should be considered from first the patient's side, and second our side. **First**, if you want to know what ails a person, recognize his most dominant characteristic. It will stand out so conspicuously that, try as he may, he cannot hide it. For example, a proud person will reveal pride, even though he will try to conceal it with a cloak of humility. With a sad person, a note of sadness pervades even his laughter. Invariably, the nature of a person will leave a certain definite impression.

There are many references in the Bible describing different types of conditions in the human spirit. Some people have an impatient spirit, others an inflexible spirit, and still others have a contrite spirit. We can also say one has an arrogant spirit, another has a depressed spirit, and so forth. From where do these different conditions of the spirit come? For instance, from where does the inflexibility in a stubborn spirit come? From where comes the arrogance in a proud spirit? Surely our human spirit in its normal state is not tinged with anything. It is designed just to manifest the pure Spirit of God. How can it be, then, that the spirit is spoken of as hard or inflexible? Proud? Arrogant? Unforgiving? And jealous? The answer is this: When the outward and inward man are not divided, the condition of the outward man thus becomes mingled with that of the inward. The spirit is inflexible because it is clothed in the inflexibility of the outward man. The spirit is proud because it is clothed with the arrogance of the outward man. The spirit is jealous because of the envy of the outward man. Originally, the spirit is neutral in nature, but it can take on the character of the outward man if the latter is not broken.

Our spirit emanates from God. Originally, it was pure before it was affected and sometimes infected by the impure state of the outward man. But it becomes proud, inflexible, or whatever, wholly because of the unbrokenness of the outward man. How the outward man with its various conditions has so tainted the spirit that these conditions come forth with the spirit! Therefore, to purify the spirit, one must deal not with the spirit, but with the outward man. We must realize that the trouble lies not with the spirit, but with the outward man. From the kind of spirit released and flowing forth, we can detect immediately the area wherein a man has not been broken. The obvious kind of condition found in the outward man characterizes the type of spirit we contact.

Once we have learned to touch a man's spirit, we will know exactly what is his need. This secret of knowing man is by touching his spirit—in sensing what it is clothed with. Let us repeat emphatically this basic principle for knowing another man: It is by sensing or touching his spirit. As the spirit flows forth, it reveals either the broken or unbroken traits of the outward man. The human spirit takes its color from the outward man when it flows through the outward man.

When someone is strong in a particular point, it is like a glaring thing before you. It is so blatantly obvious that it seems you can just reach out and touch it. If you feel it, you know what it is. You will then realize that this thing is his unbroken outward man. If you can sense a man's spirit, you will know his condition. You will know what he is attempting to reveal, or what he is trying to conceal. So we say again, if you want to know man, you must know him according to his human spirit.

Our Own Preparation for Knowing Man

Secondly, let us now consider our part in knowing man. The disciplinary measures the Holy Spirit takes with us are the God-given lessons by which He uses one thing after another until we are broken. It takes many breakings in many areas of our lives for us to attain to a place of usefulness. When we say we can touch another through the spirit, it does **not** mean that we can similarly touch **all** individuals alike, **nor** that we can discern someone's **total** spiritual condition. It is simply in the particular area where we have been disciplined by the Holy Spirit and broken by the Lord that we can touch another. If we have not been broken by the Lord in a particular thing, we can in no wise supply that need to our Christian brother. In those very points, our spirit is insensitive and impotent.

Here is invariably a spiritual fact: Our spirit is released according to the degree of our brokenness. The one who has accepted the most discipline is the one who can best serve. The more one is broken, the more sensitive he can be. The more loss one has suffered, the more he has to give. Wherever we save ourselves, it is at that very place where we become spiritually useless. Whenever we preserve and excuse ourselves, it is at that point where we are deprived of spiritual sensitivity and supply. Let no one imagine he can be effective if he disregards this basic principle.

Only those who have learned some lessons can serve. You may learn ten years' lessons in one year, or you may take twenty or thirty years to learn one year's lessons. Any delay in learning means a delay in serving. If God has put a desire in your heart to serve Him, you should understand what is involved. The way of service lies in brokenness and is connected with your accepting the discipline of the Holy Spirit. The measure of your service is determined by the depth of discipline and brokenness. Be assured that human emotions or cleverness cannot help. How much you really possess is based upon how much God has wrought in your life. Therefore, the more you are dealt with, the keener is your perception of man. The more you are disciplined by the Holy Spirit, the more readily your spirit can touch another.

It is very important to remember that while God's Spirit is **given** to us believers once for all, we must go on **learning** what was given in our spirit throughout our lifetime. Thus, the more we learn, the more we can discern. It is a source of grief to us that so many Christian brothers and sisters in the Lord do not know how to exercise spiritual discernment. Too many fail to differentiate between what is of the Lord and what is of their human nature. Only as we have experienced the Lord's strict dealing with us in certain personal matters can we quickly detect it in others, like detecting early sprouts from hidden seeds. We do not need to wait for it to grow until fruit is manifested. We can discern it long before harvest time. So our spiritual sensitivity is gradually gained through the personal experience of God's hand upon us.

For example, someone may mentally condemn pride, yes, even preach against it. However, he has no sense of the sinfulness of pride in his own spirit. Hence, his spirit is not distressed when pride appears in his brother. He may even be sympathetic. Then, the day comes when God's Spirit so works in his life that he really sees the

51

ugliness of pride. He is dealt with by God, and his pride is consumed. Although his preaching against pride may sound the same as before, yet now every time a spirit of pride appears in his brother, he senses its ugliness and is thereby distressed. What he has learned and seen from God for himself enables him to discern it and be distressed about it in his brother. In fact, such a sense of "distress" most suitably describes his inward sensitivity. Now that he recognizes his own ailment, he can now serve his brother. Once he was attacked by the same affliction; now he is somewhat cured. This does not imply that he should claim complete deliverance simply that he knows some measure of cure. Therefore, the experiences of lessons learned demonstrate how we come into the reality of spiritual understanding and discernment.

Spiritual sensitivity comes about only through many dealings. Does sparing ourselves really profit us? *"For whosoever shall save his life shall lose it."* Ask not the Lord to withdraw His hand from us. How tragic it is not to recognize what the Lord is doing. We may even be unwittingly resisting His hand. The absence of spiritual understanding is due to the lack of learning spiritual lessons. Therefore, let us realize that the more we are dealt with, the better we shall know men, discern things, and supply the needs of others. No other way than the way of the Lord's dealings with us can enlarge the sphere of our service and broaden the scope of our experiences.

Learning How To Practice It

Once these basic lessons have been learned, we find our spirit is released and better able to pinpoint the real conditions of others. Now, how can we put this into practice?

First, to touch a man's spirit, we must wait until he opens his mouth and talks. Few ever arrive at the place where they can touch a man's spirit without first hearing **how** he speaks. The Word of God says: *"For out of the abundance of the heart the mouth speaks"* (Matt. 12:34). Whatever his real intentions may be, his spirit is revealed by **how**, not what, he speaks through his mouth. If he is arrogant, a proud spirit will manifest itself through his words. If hypocritical, a flattering spirit will be evident in his speech. Or, if envious, a jealous spirit will be displayed through his conversations. As you listen to him speak, you will touch his spirit. Do not merely pay attention to what he says, but especially note the condition of his spirit. We know man, not only by the words of his mouth, but also by the tone of his spirit.

On one occasion, when the Lord Jesus was traveling toward Jerusalem, two of His disciples saw the Samaritans refusing to receive Him. They questioned Him: *"Lord, wilt Thou that we command fire to come down from heaven and consume them as also Elias did?"* (Luke 9:54). As they were speaking, their spirit was exposed. The Lord's reply was, *"Ye know not of what **spirit** ye are"* (9:55). The Lord shows us here that by listening to a man's words, you will know what kind of spirit he expresses. As soon as the disciples's words were uttered, their spirit was exhibited, *"for out of the abundance of the heart the mouth speaks."*

There is yet a **second** point to bear in mind. When you are listening to a conversation, do not allow the topic under discussion to distract you from the spirit with which he speaks. Suppose two brothers are involved in a quarrel, each one blaming the other. If this matter is brought to you, how are you to deal with it? Although you may have no objective way of checking out the facts if only the two of them were present, you do know however that as soon as they open their mouths, their spirits are revealed. Right or wrong among Christians is judged, not only by their action, but also by the tenor of their spirit which is inflected by their voice. When a brother starts to talk, you may sense immediately that his spirit is wrong, though you may lack the necessary factual information about the case. One brother may complain that the other berated and lambasted him, but immediately you sense his spirit is not right! The real issue therefore is with the condition of the spirit—not what he says, but how he says it.

Before God, the merits of a case are determined not so much by whether the deeds are right or wrong, but whether the **spirit** is right or wrong. How often in the church a wrong deed is accompanied by a wrong spirit. But if judgment is made solely according to outward deeds, we have dragged the church into another realm. We should be in the realm of the inward spirit, not merely of outward action.

Once our own spirit has been released, we can detect the condition of others' spirits. If we contact a closed and locked up spirit, we have to exercise our spirit in judging the issue and discerning the man. May we be able to say with Paul, *"We henceforth know no one according to the flesh"* (2 Cor. 5:16). We do not know man according to his outward flesh, but according to his inner spirit. Having learned this basic lesson, we provide a way for God to work out His purpose through us.

The ministry of reconciliation 2 co5:18-21

5

The Church
and
God's Work

IF WE REALLY UNDERSTAND the nature of God's work, we shall readily admit that the outward man is truly a formidable hindrance. Surely, God is considerably restricted by man. When the people of God acknowledge this, they will be ready to know the ultimate purpose of the church and its correlation with God's power and God's work.

God's Manifestation and God's Restriction

There came a time when God committed Himself to human form in the Person of Jesus of Nazareth. Before the Word became flesh, God's fullness knew no bounds. Once the incarnation became a reality, God's work and God's power were limited to the channel of His flesh. The question then was this: Will this Man, Jesus Christ,

55

restrict or manifest God? We are shown from the Bible that, far from limiting God, He has incredibly manifested God's fullness. The rich fullness of God was channeled, without restriction, through His flesh. Hence, His flesh contained the unrestricted fullness of God's life and power.

However, in our day God commits Himself to the church. Currently, His power and His work flows in and through the church. Just as in the Gospels where we find all of God's work given to the Son, so today God has entrusted all His work to the church and will not act apart from it. From the Day of Pentecost up to the present time, God's work has been carried out corporately through the church. Think of the church's tremendous responsibility. God's commitment to the church is like His previous commitment—without reservation or restriction—to the one Man, Christ. However, the church may restrict God's work or limit His manifestation.

Jesus of Nazareth was God Himself. His whole being, from within to without, revealed God. His emotions reflected God's emotions. His thoughts manifested God's thoughts. While on this earth, He could say: *"Not that I should do My will, but the will of Him that has sent Me. The Son can do nothing of Himself save whatever He sees the Father doing.... For I have not spoken from Myself, but the Father who sent Me has Himself given Me commandment what I should say and what I should speak"* (Jn. 6:38; 5:19; 12:49). Here we see a Man unto Whom God is totally committed. He is the Word that became flesh. He is God becoming man. He is perfect. So the day came when God desired to distribute His life to men, and this Man could declare: *"The grain of wheat falling into the ground... if it die... bears much fruit"* (Jn. 12:24). Moreover, God has chosen the church to be His collective vessel today—the vessel of His speaking and for the manifestation of His power and His working.

The basic teaching of the Gospels portrays the presence of God **in one Man**, while that of the Epistles declares God through many members **in the church**. May our eyes be opened to this glorious

56

fact: God formerly dwelt in the Man Jesus Christ, but now God is only in the church as the vehicle of His purpose, not in any other lesser thing.

When this light dawns on us, we will spontaneously lift up our eyes to heaven and say, "Oh, God! How much we have hindered Thee!" In Christ, the Almighty God was still almighty without suffering any restriction or constraints. What God expects today is that this same power may remain intact as He resides in the church. God should be as free in manifesting Himself in the church as He was in Christ. Any impediment or disability in the church will invariably limit God. This is a most serious thing. We do not mention it lightly. The hindrance in each of us constitutes a hindrance to God.

Why is the discipline of the Holy Spirit so important? Why is the dividing of spirit and soul so urgent? It is because God must have a free flowing way through us. Let no one think that we are only interested in individual spiritual experience. Our concern is the release of God's way and the liberty of His work in the Body. Is God free to work through our lives? Unless we, through the Spirit's discipline, are dealt with and broken, we shall restrict God. Without the breaking of the outward man, the church cannot be a channel for God.

Breaking—God's Way of Working

Let us now proceed to consider how the breaking of the outward man will affect us: First, our reading of God's Word. Second, our ministering of His Word. And third, our preaching the Gospel.

1—**Reading the Bible:** It is beyond question that 'what we are' determines what we get out of the Bible. How often man in his conceit hangs onto his unrenewed and confused mind by which he reads the Bible. The consequence of this is nothing but his own thought. He does not touch the Spirit of the Holy Scriptures. If we expect to meet the Lord in His Word, our contentious thoughts must first be broken by God. We may think highly of our brilliant opinion, but to God, it is a great obstacle. Our originality can never lead us into God's thought.

There are at least two basic requirements for reading the Bible: First, our thought must enter into **the thought of the Bible**. And second, our spirit must enter into **the Spirit of the Bible**. You must think as the writer—whether it be Paul, Peter, or John—when he had written God's Word. So **firstly**, your thought must begin where his thought begins, and develop as his develops. You must be able to reason as he reasons and to exhort as he exhorts. In other words, your thought must be geared to his thought. This will allow the Holy Spirit to give you the precise meaning of the Scriptures.

Think of a person coming to the Bible with his mind already set. He reads the Bible to get support for his preconceived doctrines. How tragic! An experienced person, after hearing such a one speak for five or ten minutes, can discern whether the speaker is using the Bible for his own ends or has his deliberation been integrated into the thought of the Bible. There is a range of difference here. One may stand up and give a pleasing and seemingly scriptural message, but actually his thought is inconsistent with the thought of the Bible. Or we may hear someone preach wherein his thought expresses the thought of the Bible and is therefore harmonious and united with it. Although this condition should be the norm, not all have reached it. Integrating our thought with the thought of the Bible necessitates the breaking of the outward man. Do not think our Bible reading is poor because of a lack of instruction. The defect is rather in us, because our opinionated thoughts have not been subdued by God. So brokenness will cause us to cease from our own independent opinions and subjective thinking. Then gradually we will begin to touch the mind of the Lord and follow the trend of thought inherent in the Bible. Not until the outward man is broken can we enter into the thought of God's Word.

Now while this is important, we have yet to mention the primary matter. The Bible is more than words, ideas, and thoughts. So this brings us to the **second** requirement in reading the Bible. The most outstanding feature of the Bible is that God's Spirit is released through this Book. When one of the writers—whether Peter, John, Matthew, or Mark—is inspired by the Holy Spirit, not only does his renewed mind follow the inspired thought, but also his spirit is released along with the Holy Spirit. The world cannot understand that there is the Spirit in God's Word, and that this Spirit can be released through our spirit, just as it was manifested in the ministry of the prophet. Today, if you were listening to a prophet's message, you will realize that there is a mysterious 'something' other than mere words and thoughts present. This 'something' you can clearly sense, and we may well call it the Spirit in God's Word.

Not only is there **firstly** the Divine **Thought** in the Bible, but **secondly** the Divine **Spirit** is also therein present, waiting to come forth from the Bible. Thus, it is only when your human spirit is released and can touch the Spirit of the Bible that you can understand what the Bible says. To illustrate, let us think of a naughty boy who deliberately breaks a neighbor's window. The neighbor comes out and gives him quite a tongue-lashing. But when the boy's mother learns of his mischief, she also rebukes him severely. But somehow there is a difference in the spirit between the two scoldings. The one is ill-tempered, given in an angry spirit. But the mother's discipline expresses love, hope, and training. This is just a simple example. The Spirit who inspires the Scriptures is the eternal Spirit and is ever present in the Bible for our good. If our outward man has been broken, our human spirit is released and can thereby touch the loving, hopeful, and helpful inspiration of the Spirit contained in the Scriptures. Otherwise, the Bible will remain like a dead book in our hands, especially if the mind of our outward man is not broken and the condition of our spirit is not released.

2—Ministering the Word: First, God desires that we understand His Word, and this is the starting point of our spiritual service. Second, He is equally desirous to put His Word as a burden in our spirit so that we may use it to minister to the church. In Acts 6:4 we read, *"But we will give ourselves up to prayer and the ministry of the Word." "Ministry"* means serving. So the ministry of the Word means serving people with the Word of God.

What is the difficulty in our ministry, especially when we experience failure to release the Word from within us? Often one may be heavily burdened with a Word which he feels ought to be communicated to the brethren. However, as he stands to speak sentence after sentence, the inner burden remains as heavy as ever. Even after an hour has passed, there is no sense of relief. Finally, he departed, remaining as heavily burdened as when he came. Why? It is because his outward man had not been broken and had failed therefore to give utterance to his burden. Instead of his soul faculties giving help, they have become an obstacle to the inward man.

Yet once the outward man is broken, utterance is no longer a problem. One can then release the appropriate words to express his inner feeling. Once our words are released through our spirit, the inner burden is lightened. This is the way to minister God's Word to the church. So we repeat: The outward man is the greatest hindrance to the ministry of the Word of God.

Many have the erroneous notion that capable, clever people are the best endowed ones to be useful to the Lord. How wrong! No matter how clever you are, the outward can never substitute the inward man. Only after the outward man is broken can the inward find adequate thoughts and appropriate words. The shell of the outward man must be smashed by God. The more it is shattered, the more the life in our spirit is released. As long as this outer shell remains unbroken and intact, the burden in the spirit cannot be released, nor can God's life and power flow from you to the church. It is mostly through the ministry of God's Word that His life and power are supplied. Unless your inward man is released, people will only hear the sound of your voice. They cannot touch life. You may have a word to give, but others fail to receive it, because you have no clear, meaningful utterance.

The difficulty is that the life within fails to flow out. There is a word from God moving within your spirit, yet it cannot be manifested, because of the outward obstacle of the outward man. God does not have a free way in and through you.

3—**Preaching the Gospel:** Here is a common misconception—people think they have belief in the Gospel because they have been either mentally convinced of its doctrinal correctness or emotionally excited by its appeal. But in actual fact, those who respond to the Gospel for either of these two reasons do not last long. Yes, the intellect and emotions need to be reached, but these alone are insufficient. Mind may reach mind, and emotions may reach emotions, but salvation probes much deeper. The divine Spirit must touch the human spirit. Only when the spirit of the preacher shines and blossoms forth do sinners fall down and capitulate to God. This is the released spirit necessary for preaching the Gospel.

A miner, greatly used by God, wrote a book called SEEN AND HEARD, in which he relates his experiences in preaching the Gospel. We were deeply touched by reading his book. Although just an ordinary brother, neither highly educated nor especially gifted, he offered himself wholly to the Lord and was mightily used. The one thing that characterized him was that he was a broken man, allowing his spirit to emerge easily. While in a meeting and listening to a preacher, he was so burdened for souls that he asked the preacher for permission to speak. He went to the pulpit, but no words came. His inner man was so burning with a passion for souls that his tears gushed forth in torrents. In all, he managed to utter just a few incoherent sentences. Yet God's Spirit filled that meeting place; and people were convicted of their sins and their fallen condition. Here was a young man who was broken. He had few words. But when his spirit came forth, people were mightily moved. In reading his autobiography, we recognize that here was one whose spirit was wholly released. He was instrumental for saving many during his lifetime.

This is the way to preach the Gospel. Whenever you see someone who is unsaved, you sense you should give him the Gospel. But you must allow your spirit to be released. To preach the Gospel is purely a matter of having the outward man broken so that the inward man can flow forth and touch others. When your spirit touches another's spirit, God's Spirit is actually flowing through the channel of your spirit. Consequently, the Holy Spirit quickens or enlivens the deadened spirit of sinners, who are in darkness, so that they may be wonderfully saved. However, if your spirit is obstructed by the outward man, God has no outlet in you and the Gospel is blocked. This is why we focus so much attention on the dealing with the outward man. If we lack that dealing, we are powerless to win souls, though we may have memorized all the doctrines . Salvation comes when our spirit touches another's spirit. Then that soul cannot but prostrate himself at God's feet. Oh, beloved, when our spirit is truly released, souls will surely be saved.

Once people are saved, God does not want them to wait before they deal with their sins. And then wait for a few more years before they are consecrated. And still wait longer before they answer the call to really follow the Lord. As soon as people believe, they should immediately turn from their sins, consecrate themselves wholly to the Lord, and break the power of mammon. Their story should be like those recorded in the Gospels and in the Acts. For the Gospel to have its fullest effect in man, the Lord must channel a passageway through the lives of these messengers of the Gospel.

In these years we have been wholly convinced that the Lord is working toward a fuller recovery. For instance, the Gospel of grace and the Gospel of the kingdom must be joined together   In the

Gospels, these two were never separated. Only in later years does it seem as if those who have heard the Gospel of grace know little or nothing of the Gospel of the kingdom. Thus, the two have been separated. But the time is now ripe for both Gospels to be united, so that people can become thoroughly saved, forsaking everything, and wholly consecrating themselves to the Lord.

Let us bow our heads before the Lord and acknowledge that the Gospel must be fully preached and its messengers be fully dealt with. For the Gospel to enter into men, we must allow God to manifest Himself through us. Just as an effective preaching of the Gospel requires more power, so the messengers of the Gospel must pay a higher price. We must put everything on the altar. Let us pray as follows: "Lord, I put my all on the altar. Cut a way through me so that the church may find a way. I would not be one who both blocks You and thus blocks the church."

The Lord Jesus never restricted God in any way. For nearly two thousand years, God has been working in the church, ever pressing towards the day when the church will no longer restrict Him. As Christ fully manifests God, so likewise shall the church. Step by step, God is instructing and dealing with His children. Again and again, we sense His hand upon us. So shall it be until the day arrives when the church is indeed the full manifestation of God. Today, let us turn to the Lord and confess: "Lord, we are ashamed. We have delayed Your work. We have hindered Your life. We have blocked the spread of the Gospel. And we have limited Your power." Individually, in our hearts, let us commit ourselves to Him afresh, saying: "Lord, I put my all on the altar, that Thou may have a channel in and through me."

If we expect the effectiveness of the Gospel to be fully recovered, our consecration must be thorough. We must consecrate ourselves to God even like those in the early church. May God have an outlet through us.

6

Brokenness
and
Discipline

Consecration Basic to Brokenness

FOR THE BREAKING of the outward man, a full consecration is imperative. However, we must also understand that this crisis act of consecration alone will not solve the whole problem of service. Consecration is merely an expression of our unqualified willingness to be categorically in the hands of God. And it can take place in just a few minutes. Do not think God can do a quick work and finish His dealings with us in a short time. Although we are willing to offer ourselves completely to God, it is merely a start on our spiritual pilgrimage. It is like entering the gate. After the **gateway** of consecration, there is the long

pathway of the discipline of the Holy Spirit. It takes an initial consecration **plus** the persistent discipline of the Holy Spirit to make us vessels prepared for the Master's use. However, without consecration, the Holy Spirit will encounter a difficult time in His discipline of our outer man. But remember that our consecration will never serve as a substitute for His discipline.

Here then is a vital distinction: Our consecration can only be according to our **limited** insight and understanding, but the Holy Spirit's discipline is according to God's own **unlimited** light. We really do not know to what extent our consecration should entail. Our light, though so limited, seems to us to be somewhat the brightest. But in God's view, when our light is compared with His own light, it will seem like pitch-blackness. Hence, the light of God's requirement exceeds far beyond our consecration under our diminished light. The discipline of the Holy Spirit, on the other hand, is parceled out to us according to God's own light. He knows our special need, and His Spirit orders our circumstances accordingly to bring about the breaking of the outward man. Remember this: The discipline of the Holy Spirit transcends far beyond our consecration.

Since the Holy Spirit works according to God's light, His discipline is thorough and complete, because it is according to what God sees. We often wonder at the things which happen to us. Yet if left to ourselves, we could very easily make mistaken choices for our lives. So the discipline He ordains transcends our puny understanding. How often we are suddenly caught unprepared in some uneventful crisis and conclude that surely this is not what we needed. Many times His discipline descends upon us suddenly, without the warning of any prior notice! We may insist we are living in "the light," but the Holy Spirit is dealing with us according to God's light. From the time we received Him, He has been ordering our circumstances for our best profit according to His complete knowledge of us.

The working of the Holy Spirit in our lives has its positive as well as its negative sides—both constructive and destructive phases. After we were born again, we received the indwelling life of the Holy Spirit. But our outward man, however, often deprives Him of His freedom to move and work in our lives. It is like trying to walk in a pair of ill-fitted new shoes. Because our outward is in conflict with our inward man, God must employ whatever means He thinks effective in breaking down any stubborn stronghold over which our inward man has no control.

The Holy Spirit does not break the outward man by simply supplying more grace to the inward man. Of course, God wants the inward man to be strong. But His method for diminishing the outward man is by utilizing external means. It would be well nigh impossible for the inward man to accomplish this. Both the inward and the outward are so different in nature that they can scarcely inflict any wounds on each other. The nature of both the outward man and external things are similar; therefore, the former can easily be affected by the latter. External things can strike and bruise the outward man most painfully. So it is the external things that God uses to deal with our outward man.

You remember the Bible says that two sparrows are sold for a farthing (Matt. 10:29) and that five sparrows are sold for two farthings (Lk. 12:6). This is certainly cheap, and the fifth sparrow is included free. However, *"one of them shall not fall to the ground without your Father; but even the hairs of your head are all numbered"* (Matt. 10:29, 30). Not only is every hair **counted**, but every single one is also **numbered**. Therefore, we say this to assure you that all of our circumstances likewise are sovereignly ordered by God. Nothing is accidental.

God's ordering is according to His knowledge of our need. He has in view the shattering of our outward man. Knowing that some external thing will in particular affect us, God will arrange for it to encounter us once, twice, and thrice again. Do you not realize that all the events of your life for the past five or ten years were ordered by God for your education? If you murmured and complained, you have grievously failed to recognize His hand. If you thought you were just unfortunate and unlucky, you are ignorant of the Holy Spirit's discipline. Remember that whatever happens to us is measured by the hand of God for our supreme good. Although we might not choose it, God knows what is best for us. Where would we be today if God had not so disciplined us through the ordering of our circumstances? It is this very thing which keeps us pure and keeps us walking in His pathway. How foolish are those who have murmurings on their tongues and fires of contention and resentment smouldering in their hearts at the very predicaments the Holy Spirit has measured to them for their good.

As soon as we are saved, the Holy Spirit begins to dole out discipline. But He cannot act to deal freely until our consecration is complete. After one is saved and is not yet consecrated, he still loves himself much more than the Lord. Nonetheless, the Holy Spirit is working continually to bring him under control and to break down his outward man until He may work without any hindrance.

Finally, there comes a time when you realize that you cannot live **by** yourself and **for** yourself. Even in the dimmed light of your understanding, you should come to God and say: "I consecrate myself to You. Come life or death, I have committed myself totally into Your hands." This will strengthen the work of the Holy Spirit in your life. Herein lies the importance of consecration: It allows the Holy Spirit to work without restriction. So think it not strange when many unexpected things plague you after your consecration.

Eventually, you will tell the Lord: "Lord! Do whatever You consider best in my life." Now that you have put yourself unconditionally into His hands, the Holy Spirit will now take you over and work freely in your life. Now that you decide wholeheartedly to follow the Lord without any resistence, you must pay close attention to the disciplinary work of the Holy Spirit.

The Greatest Means of Grace

God has been bestowing His grace upon us from the day we were saved. The ways by which we may receive grace from God are called "**the means of grace**." Prayer and listening to a message are two examples, for through them we can draw near to God and receive grace. This descriptive term, "the means of grace," has been universally accepted by the Church down through the centuries. It refers to the grace received by means of meetings, messages, prayers, and so forth. But surely the greatest means of grace which we cannot afford to neglect is the discipline of the Holy Spirit. Nothing can be compared with this means of grace—not prayers, not Bible readings, not meetings, not messages, not meditation, not even hymns of praise. Among all of the God-given means of grace, it would seem the discipline of the Holy Spirit is the most important.

Looking back over our Christian life, we can trace this one specific means of grace in our many experiences. By this one means, we can see how far we have profitably advanced with the Lord. What we experience daily—at home, in school, during working hours, or on the road—it is all ordered by the Holy Spirit for our maximum benefit. If we have not profited by this one outstanding means of grace, we suffer terrible loss. None of the other means can replace it, precious though they all are. Messages feed us, prayer restores us, God's Word refreshes us, fellowship with others encourages us, and helping others liberates us. But should our outward man remain strong, we give all who contact us the impression of having mixed and impure motives. People will recognize our zeal, but also our ambitious self. They will see our love toward the Lord, but also love for ourselves. They feel we are a precious brother, yet a difficult one. All because our outward man has not been broken. Let us not forget that though we are built up through messages, prayer, and the Bible, yet the greatest means of edification is the discipline of the Holy Spirit.

69

Henceforth, there must be on our part a more complete consecration so that we will submit to what the Holy Spirit arranges. Much submission will bring much blessing to us. If, instead, we quarrel with God and follow our own stubborn inclinations, we shall miss this way of His higher blessing. Once we realize that all of God's arrangements are for our highest profit—even things that are troublesome to us—and are willing to accept them as disciplinary measures **from Him**, we shall see how the Holy Spirit will make use of all things in His dealing with us.

Dealings of Various Kinds

If material things entangle you, God is faithful to deal with them one after another. Not even such trivialities as food and clothing can escape the careful hand of the Holy Spirit. He will not neglect one area in your life. You may even be ignorant of your affinity for certain things, but He knows you and will deal with it most thoroughly. Not until the day comes when all these things are stripped away will you know perfect liberty. In all of these dealings you will finally recognize the thoroughness of the Holy Spirit. Even things long forgotten are brought to your mind by the Lord. Perfect is God's wonderful work, and nothing less than perfection can satisfy Him. He cannot stop short.

Sometimes He will deal with you through your relationships with others. He will arrange for you to remain with someone you cannot escape. Someone who made you angry. Someone whom you despised. Or, someone who made you jealous. Very often these dealings come through the ones you love. Before, you did not know how unclean and mixed your selfish attitudes were. But afterwards, you realize how much "rubbish" still exists in you. You had thought you were wholly and absolutely for the Lord. But after receiving the discipline of the Holy Spirit, you begin to see the far-reaching effects that those external things have upon your life.

Moreover, the hand of God may touch our thought life. We discover that our thoughts are often confused, individualistic, selfish, and uncontrollable. We pretend to be wiser than others. Then the Lord allows us to crash into a wall and hit the dust—all to show us that we dare not use our thoughts inordinately. Once we have been enlightened in this area of our life, we shall fear our own thoughts like fire. Just like a hand quickly pulled back from a flaming fire, so we shall instantly draw back when we encounter our unmanageable thoughts. We constantly remind ourselves, "This is not what I should think. I am afraid to pursue my own thoughts."

Furthermore, God will so arrange our circumstances to work on our emotional life. Some people are extremely emotional. When they are elated, they cannot contain themselves. When they are depressed, they cannot be comforted. Their whole life revolves around their roller-coaster emotions, with their elation resulting in feverish activities and their depression in passivity. How does God rectify this? He places them in situations where they dare be neither too happy when elated, nor too sad when depressed. They can only depend upon the grace of God and live by His mercy, not by their fickle emotions.

Although difficulties with thoughts and emotions are quite common, the greatest and most prevalent difficulty however is with the will. Our emotions run wild because our wills have not been dealt with. The root of our troublesome emotions is in our will. The same is true with our thoughts. We may be able to mouth the words, *"Not my will but Thine be done,"* but how often do we really allow the Lord to take over when things happen? The less you know yourself, the more you will easily utter such words. The less enlightened you are about yourself, the more submissive to God you appear to be in your own eyes. He who speaks easily and cheaply has proven that he has never paid the price.

Only after God works on us do we really see how our wills are so very stubborn, and we find it too handy to cover them up with our excuses and opinions. God must deal with us until our wills are submissive and manageable. Strong-willed people are convinced that their feelings, ways, and judgments are always right. Consider how Paul received this grace as recorded in Philippians: *"Have no confidence in the flesh"* (3:3). Be willing to allow God to lead you to such a place when you dare not trust in your own judgment. God will allow us to make mistake after mistake until we realize that this will be a constant pattern in the future. We truly need the grace of the Lord. Frequently, the Lord permits us to reap serious consequences from our own self-assertive judgments.

Finally, you will be so stricken by your failures until you will say: "I fear my own judgment like I fear the fires of hell. Lord, I am so prone to mistakes. Unless You are merciful to me, unless You support me, unless You restrain me with Your hand, I will blunder again." This is the beginning of the defeat of the outward man—when you no longer dare to trust yourself. Your opinions usually have come so easily, until God has repeatedly dealt with you and caused you to have suffered many failures. Finally, you yield, and say: "God, I dare not think about things without You; I dare not decide things without You." This is the discipline of the Holy Spirit—when all kinds of things and all sorts of people are pressing in on you from all directions.

Do not think there will ever be any letup of this lesson! Very often the supply of God's Word is lacking, or some other means of grace is insufficient, yet this one special means of grace—the discipline of the Holy Spirit—is ever with us. You may say you have no opportunity to hear and be supplied by His Word. But this can never be true of the discipline of the Holy Spirit. Daily, He is arranging ample opportunities for you to learn.

Once you yield yourself to God, you will discover that His discipline will meet your need to a far greater magnitude than the

72

supply of His Word. This is not just for the learned, the clever, or the gifted. No, it is the ordained way for every child of God. The supply of God's Word, the power of prayer, the encouragement of fellowship among the believers—none of them qualify as a substitute for the discipline of the Holy Spirit. Why is this? It is because you need not only to be built up; you need also to be **broken down**. You need to be delivered of all the many present things today, because they are not found in eternity.

The Cross in Operation

The cross is more than a mere doctrine. It is something that is already in practice. Do not think that the way to humility is some self-exerted effort to remind ourselves constantly never to be proud. We must be stricken again and again—even if it means twenty times—until we surrender to the circumstances God ordered to break our pride. Let us never assume this comes about by merely following the teaching of a certain leader. No, this will never work, because our pride can only be broken by God's dealing.

Through the operation of the cross, we shall learn to **depend** upon the grace of God, not on our memory. Whether we remember it or not, the fact remains: He is accomplishing a work which is dependable and lasting. Formerly, the outward and the inward man were not able to join hands. But now the outward man waits meekly in fear and trembling before God, and is subsequently no longer in conflict with the inner man.

Everyone of us needs the discipline of dealings from the Lord. As we review our past history, can we not but see the hand of God in dealing with the independence, pride, and selfishness of our outward man? We have now discovered how everything that has ever happened to us is so very meaningful.

7

Dividing and Revelation

GOD DESIRES <u>firstly</u> to **break** down the outward man, and <u>secondly</u> to **separate** it so that the inward man may no longer be entangled and mixed in with the outward man's activities. Or, we may simply say about this second point, God wants to divide our spirit from our soul.

How rare it is in these days to find an unmixed and pure spirit. Usually, whenever our spirit comes forth, it does so with our soul, because they are mixed. So another basic requirement in God's work is a **pure** spirit—not a powerful spirit. Those who neglect this will find their work damaged, though it is done with much power, due to the lack of the purity of spirit. Although they may truly possess the power of God, yet because their spirit is mixed with the natural powers of their soul, they are wrecking what they build. Let us see if we can understand how this is.

Some may think that as long as they receive power from God, all of their natural abilities originate from God. But this is not so! The more we know God, the more we will know and love a pure spirit—a purity which allows no intermingling of the outward man with the inward. One whose outward man has not been dealt with cannot expect the power of life that flows from within him to be pure. For this, spiritual power is nothing but a mingled mixture when it is channeled through his unbroken self, though it may have apparently good results. It nevertheless constitutes a sin before God.

Many young brothers, knowing full well that the Gospel is the power of God, still insinuate the influence of their own cleverness, their witty jests, and their personal feelings into their preaching of the Gospel. Consequently, people touch their self as well as God's power. Although these evangelists may not sense it, others who are pure in spirit will instantly detect such mixed impurities. How often our zeal in Gospel endeavors is mixed with what attracts us naturally. We are doing the will of God because it happens to coincide with our preferences and wills. Hence, in standing firm and strong for God, we are merely expressing our strong and willful personality. No matter how good the soul's powers may appear, the mere mixture of these powers with the spirit's life is considered impure and sinful before the eyes of God.

Since our greatest problem is this impure mixture, God must do a work in our lives beyond the breaking of our outward man. He must also purify and refine our outward man from the mixtures which God considers as impurities. While God is breaking our hard outer shell, He is also at the same time doing the work of refining. Thus, we see His **two-fold dealings** with us: **the breaking down of the outward man, and the dividing of it from the spirit**. The first is done through the discipline of the Holy Spirit, while the second is accomplished through the Spirit's revelation.

The Necessity of both a Broken and Divided Work

Therefore, the outward man has two separate needs. First, the outward man needs to be broken in order to release the spirit. Second, when the spirit does come forth, it must not be clouded or muddied by the outward man. This problem takes us further than the mere release of the spirit. It also touches upon the human spirit's clearness and purity.

If one is not enlightened as to the self-centered nature of his outward man, and does not judge it strictly before God, instinctively his outward man will involuntarily come out mixed together with his spirit. While he is ministering before God, we can tell that some form of self has come out. He may express God, but he also expresses his unjudged self. Is it not strange that the most dominant characteristic of our personality always touches others? This is the unjudged part of our outward man who will project his strongest natural trait to others. This is beyond anyone's pretension. How can you expect to become spiritual in the pulpit if you are not spiritual in your home? Can you project yourself into spirituality? However hard you may try, your natural self stands unveiled whenever you open your mouth.

If you truly desire to be delivered, God must deal with your natural strength in a basic way, not just superficially. Only after He has broken your chief personality trait can your spirit be released without the impurities of a mixed soul being inflicted upon others.

Impure mixtures are one of the biggest problems in the lives of God's servants. Frequently, we touch both life and death in a brother. Yes, we find God, but also the self. A meek spirit, but also stubbornness. The Holy Spirit, but also the flesh—all wrapped up in the same person. When he stands up to speak, he impresses others with a spirit mixed with the powers of his soul—a spirit which is not purified. Thus, for God to use you as a minister of His Word, for you to be His mouthpiece, you must seek His favor by praying: "O God, do a work in me! Not only break my outer man, but also divide it from my inner man until it is a pure channel for my spirit." Otherwise, the Lord's Name will suffer loss. You are giving to men that which is of the self while ministering God's Word. The Lord's Name does not suffer because of your lack of life, but because of your spirit flowing with the mixture it picked up while passing through your natural soul. This mixture is what God calls unclean. Moreover, the church likewise suffers.

Now that we have considered the **discipline** of the Holy Spirit in earlier chapters, what about the **revelation** of the Holy Spirit? The discipline of the Spirit may precede His revelation, or it may follow. There is no fixed order. With some, He may begin with His discipline. In others, with His revelation. However, it is certain that the discipline of the Holy Spirit **exceeds** His revelation. We are of course referring to the experiences of God's children, and not to mere doctrine. To most, it will seem that discipline plays a more frequent and a much larger part than revelation. At any rate, through the Spirit's discipline, the shell of the outer man is **broken**. And, through the Spirit's revelation, the powers of the outer man are completely **divided** from the spirit.

How Does the Living Word Divide

"For the Word of God is living and operative, and sharper than any two-edged sword, and penetrating to the division of soul and spirit, both of joints and marrow, and a discerner of the thoughts and intents of the heart. And there is not a creature unapparent before Him; but all things are naked and laid bare to His eyes, with Whom we have to do" (Heb. 4:12,13).

The first thing to notice is that the Word of God is *"living."* His Word must surely be living if we acted on it. For if we do not find it living, we simply have failed to contact the life-power of God's Word.

We may have read over the words of the Bible, but if we do not touch something living, we have not contacted God's Word deeply enough.

John 3:16 says: *"For God so loved the world, that He gave His only begotten Son, that whosoever believes on Him may not perish, but have life eternal."* Consider how one may hear such a word. He kneels down and prays: "Lord, I thank You and praise You, for You have loved me and saved me!" We immediately know this man has touched the Word of God, for His Word has become a living reality to him. Another man may sit by his side, listening to the very same words, but he did not actually **hear** the Word of God. There is no living response from him. We can draw but one conclusion—since God's Word is living, he who listens and does not have a living response is he who has not actually heard the Word of God.

Not only is the Word of God living; it is also operative. *"Living"* points to its nature, while *"operative"* applies to its ability to fulfill its work on man. God's Word cannot return void. It will prevail and accomplish its purpose. It is not merely **a** word, but **the** Word that will so operate until it produces results.

What, then, does God's Word do for us? It penetrates and divides. It is sharper than any two-edged sword. Its sharpness is demonstrated in the *"**penetrating** to the **division** of soul and spirit, both of joints and marrow."* Note the analogy here: It compares the two-edged sword against **joints and marrow** with the Word of God against **soul and spirit**. Joints and marrow are embedded deeply into the human body. To separate the joints outside is to cut across the bones; to divide the marrow inside is to crack open the bones. Only two other things are harder to be divided than the joints and marrow—the soul and spirit. No sword, however sharp, can divide them. Similarly, we are wholly unable to distinguish between what is soul and what is spirit. Yet the Scripture tells us how the living Word of God can do the task, for it is **sharper** than any two-edged sword. God's Word is living, operative, and able to penetrate and divide. It is the soul and spirit of man which are to be penetrated and divided.

Perhaps someone may raise this question: "It doesn't seem as if the Word of God has done anything special in me. I have often heard God's Word and have even received its revelation. But I do not know what *"penetrating"* is. Nor do I understand *"division."* As far as I can tell, I am a stranger to both these processes."

How does the Bible answer this question for us? It says *"penetrating to the division of soul and spirit, both of joints and marrow."* But it also goes on to say that the Word is *"a discerner of the thoughts and intents of the heart." "Thoughts"* refers to what we deliberate in our heart, and *"intents"* have reference to our motives. Thus, the Word of God is able to discern both what we think, what motivates our thinking, and why.

Too often we can easily identify what comes from the outward man. We quite glibly confess, "This was soulish, for it came from self." But we do not really **see** what the soul or self is. Then one day, God's mercy comes to us. His light shines upon us, and His voice announces to us—with severity and solemnity: "What you frequently refer to as your "self" **is** your self! You have talked lightly and easily about the flesh. Now you must **see** how God hates this and will not allow such to continue."

Before this **seeing**, we have been able to talk facetiously about the flesh. However, once we are stricken with light, we shall confess: "Ah, this is it! This is what I have talked so lightly about!" Now, we have more than an intellectual dividing. It is the Word of God that points out and exposes what we conceived and purposed in our heart. We then receive a two-fold enlightenment: How our **thoughts** originate from the flesh, and how our **intentions** are entirely selfish.

To illustrate this, let us consider two unconverted persons. One is aware that he is a sinner. He has been to many meetings and heard many messages on sin. Clear preaching has brought him to acknowledge himself as a sinner. Yet when he accordingly refers to himself as a sinner, he laughs about it, as if it does not really matter.

The other person hears the same messages, but the light of God shines upon him. The Spirit so convicts him that he prostrates himself on the ground and prays: "Oh, yes, this is what I am—a sinner!" Not only has he **heard** it by the Word of God, but he has also **seen** and **felt** his true sinful condition. He condemns himself. He is stricken to the ground. Thus enlightened, he can confess his sin and receive the salvation of the Lord. He will henceforth never speak lightly or jokingly of the sin he has **seen**. But the first one, who can jokingly describe himself as a sinner, has not **seen** and hence is not saved.

How do you react to this message today—that your outward man seriously interferes with God and must be broken and divided by Him? If you can begin talking about it frivolously and easily, surely it has not touched you. If, on the other hand, you are enlightened by it, you will say, "O Lord, today I begin to know myself. Until now, I have not recognized my outward man." And as the light of God surrounds you, laying bare your outward man, you will fall to the ground, being no longer able to stand. Instantly, you **see** what you are.

Before, you have said that you loved the Lord. But under God's light, you find it is not so—you really love yourself. This light really divides you and sets you apart. You are inwardly separated, not by your mentality, not by mere teaching, but by God's light. Once you said you were zealous for the Lord. But now the light of God shows you that your zeal for service was entirely stirred up by your own flesh. Once you thought you loved sinners while preaching the Gospel. But now the light has come, and you discover that your preaching the Gospel stems mainly from your love of action and your love for speaking. These are merely your natural inclinations. The deeper this divine light shines, the more the thoughts and intents of your heart are revealed. Once you assumed that your thoughts and intents were of the Lord. But now in this piercing light, you know they are entirely of yourself. Such light brings you down before God.

Too often what we supposed was of the Lord proves out to be of ourselves. Although we had proclaimed that our messages were spoken by the Lord, now the light of heaven compels us to confess that the Lord has not spoken to us. Or, if He has, how little He has said. How much of the Lord's work, so called, turns out to be nothing but carnal activities! This unveiling of the real nature of things enlightens us to the true knowledge of what is of the **self** and what is of the **Lord**, how much is from our **soul** and how much is from our **spirit**. How wonderful if we can testify: His light has finally shone! The 'spirit and soul' can now be distinguished and divided! And the thoughts and intents of our heart are clearly discerned!

You who have experienced this know that this is beyond mere teaching. All efforts to distinguish between what is of self and what is of the Lord, to separate what things are of the outward man from what are of the inward man—even to the extent of listing them item by item and then memorizing them—have proven it to be nothing but a waste of time and effort. You continue to behave just as usual, for you cannot get rid of your outward man. You may even be able to condemn the flesh. You may be proud that you are able to identify what belongs to the flesh. But you are still not delivered from it.

Deliverance comes from the light of God. When the light shines, you immediately see how your denial of the flesh has been superficial and fleshly. You can even see how your criticism of the natural has been natural. But now the Lord has laid bare to your eyes the thoughts and intents of your heart. You fall prostrate before Him and say: "O Lord! Now I know these things are really from my outward man. Only Your light can really divide my outward from my inward."

Therefore, our denial of the outward man and our determination to reject it will not help. Yes, even the very confession of our sin is for naught, and our tears of repentance will need to be washed in the blood. How foolish to imagine that **we** could expose our sin! Only **in His Light** shall we see and be exposed. It must be His work by the Spirit, not our efforts by the soul. Everything out of our own mind, emotions, and will is excluded. This is something left to only God.

This is why God says, "My Word is living and effectual! My sword is the sharpest of all! When My Word comes to a man, it is able to divide the soul and spirit, just as a two-edged sword can divide the joints and marrow!"

How does it divide? It divides by revealing each thought and making bare each intention of our heart. We do not know our own heart. Beloved, only those who are in the light know their own heart. No one else does—not one! Yet when God's **living** Word comes, we then can **see**! We are exposed as one who truly **sees** his own self-centeredness—seeking only his own gratification, glory, ambition, and position for self. How blessed is that light which causes us to fall down at His feet.

What Is a Revelation?

The Scripture we have been considering continues: *"And there is not a creature unapparent before Him, but all things are naked and laid bare to His eyes, with Whom we have to do."* Here the Lord gives us the standard or criterion for dividing. What constitutes a revelation or enlightenment by the Holy Spirit? How much must we see before it is considered His revealing light? Hebrews 4:13 can help us answer this. Revelation **enables us to see what God sees.** All things are naked and laid bare before **Him**. The existence of any covering is something upon our own eyes, not God's. When God opens our eyes, we will truly know the intents of our heart and the deepest thoughts within us to the same degree as He Himself knows them—this is revelation. And, we are as naked and laid bare before Him as we are now before ourselves—again, this is revelation. ✳.Revelation allows us to see exactly what our Lord sees.

Should God be so merciful so as to grant us even a small degree of revelation—seeing ourselves as we are seen by Him—we shall immediately be smitten to the ground. We need not try to be humble. Those who live in the light cannot be proud. Only those dwelling in darkness can be proud. Outside of God's light, men can be arrogant and unapproachable. But under His revealing light, they will surely prostrate themselves before Him.

As you proceed, it becomes more evident that it is extremely difficult to explain this question of dividing the natural soul from the spiritual, the outward man from the inward spirit. Only as there is the light of revelation is the problem solved. Whenever you are enlightened to discern the thoughts and intents of your heart, you can be sure your soul and spirit are being divided.

If you desire to be used by God, sooner or later you will let His light shine upon you. You will turn to Him and say: "O God, I am absolutely unreliable. In my darkness, I do not know what I should denounce, nor what sin I should confess. Only in Thy light am I able to know what to do." Before you receive enlightenment, you may say you are a sinner, but you lack the consciousness of a sinner's contrition. You may think you hate yourself, but you have no real sense of abhorring self. You may say you deny yourself, but the feeling of abnegation is missing. Once the light comes, the veneer of pretense is stripped away and the 'real' or 'original' self is detected. What an unveiling is waiting for me—I **see** I only love myself, I **see** I deceived myself and am dishonest to the Lord, and I **see** I do not love Him. This light will pull off the mask of self which covers up who you are and what you do. Henceforth, you will have the inner knowledge of what belongs to self. Without this judgment by the light, you might even masquerade to be what you are not. But as soon as the light of God judges, your spirit and soul are divided.

What the Lord does is to pierce us with His penetrating light. It may happen while we are listening to a message, or praying by ourselves, or fellowshipping with others, or even walking alone. This incomparable light shows us how much of our words and deeds originated from ourselves. It reveals that scarcely anything that proceeded from ourselves in our Christian life and service was from the Lord. In conversation, in activities, in works, in zeal, in preaching, in helping others—in every field of life—we are devastated when we see how all-pervading is our self!

Yet once our hidden self is brought to light, the condemnation of our outward man will be spontaneous. On subsequent occasions, whenever it expresses itself, we will instantly regret it and judge it. It is only after such enlightenment that we are capable of dividing the spirit and soul. We will henceforth live before the Lord with our spirit released. It is now pure, no longer being mixed with the soul and no longer giving difficulty to the Lord.

Thus, the dividing of the spirit and soul depends upon enlightenment—being able to see as God sees. Just what does God see? He sees what we do not see. We are blind to what is of ourselves, thinking it is of God while actually it is not. What we had professed to be good is now condemned by that light. What we had considered as right, we now reject. What had passed as spiritual, we now recognize as soulish. And what we had thought was of God, we now know it to be of self. So we now confess: "Lord! Now I come to know myself as You had known me. I had been blind and self-deceived for twenty or thirty years, and to think that I did not realize it! I had not seen as You had seen."

Such a seeing delivers you from the dead weight of self. Our seeing is actually His dealing. The Word of God is effective, because it enlightens you to cast off that which is the self of the outward man. It is not that you gradually change yourself after you have heard the Word of God—as if seeing is one step and casting off another. No, enlightenment is itself a casting off. The two occur simultaneously. As soon as light strikes, the flesh is dead. No flesh can prevail in that light. The moment one comes into the light, he prostrates himself. The light has dried up his flesh. Beloved, this light is effective. Indeed, the Word of God is living and operative. God does not speak and then wait for you to make it operative. Rather, it is His Word which is effectually operative in your life.

May the Lord open our eyes to see **both** the importance of the discipline of the Holy Spirit **and** the enlightenment of His revelation. These two join hands in dealing effectively with our outward man. Let us look to the Lord for His grace to enable us to place ourselves under His light, and to be so enlightened that we might bow before Him, acknowledging: "Lord, how deceived and blind I have been all these years! I had foolishly made the mistake of confusing what came from me as flowing from You. Lord, be merciful to me!"

8

What Impression
Do We Give?

WHETHER WE CAN do the Lord's work depends not so much on our **words** or **actions**, but rather on what **impression** comes forth out of us. We are not able to edify others if we say or do one thing and some other impression is given off from our lives. It is like acting one way and living another. The strong impression emanating out of us is a very important consideration.

We often say we have a good or bad impression of someone. How do we receive such an impression? It is not just from his words, nor even from his actions. Sometimes we say, "his actions speak louder than words." But it is more than even his actions. A mysterious something expresses itself during his speaking or behavior. It is what comes out in addition to his words and deeds which gives us an impression.

The first impressions others have about us are usually what they pick up as the most outstanding trait of our personality. Take, for example, a person whose mind has never been under control and is therefore undisciplined. Spontaneously, when he begins to use his mind to contact people, they will be struck by its forcefulness. Or, if he possesses an inordinate affection, if he is overly warm or cold, others will take note of this as their first impression of him. His strongest characteristic will invariably stand out and impress others. He may be able to control his conversations and conduct, but he is unable to restrain that which expresses his nature. What he is cannot but be revealed.

II Kings 4 recounts how the Shunammite received Elisha: "*And it came to pass on a day that Elisha passed to Shunem, where there was a wealthy woman, and she constrained him to eat bread. And so it was, that as oft as he passed by, he turned in thither to eat bread. And she said to her husband, 'Behold now, I perceive that this is a holy man of God, who passes by us continually'.*" Note that Elisha preached no sermon or worked no miracle. He merely dropped in and ate a meal whenever he was passing by that way. From the way he was eating, the woman recognized him as a "*holy man of God.*" This was the impression Elisha gave to others.

We should ask ourselves: "What impression do I give to others?" How often we have emphasized the need for our outward man to be broken. If this brokenness is not accomplished, others will only be met by some peculiar deportment of our outward man. Whenever we are in others' presence, they will be made uncomfortable by our self-love, or pride, or inflexibility, or cleverness, or eloquence. Perhaps the impression we leave is a favorable one, but is God satisfied? Also, will such an impression meet the church's need? If God is not satisfied and the church is not helped, any impression we leave is not profitable.

Beloved, God's full intention requires a released spirit. Moreover, a released spirit is imperative for the growth of the church. How urgent it is, then, for our outward man to be broken! Without this breaking, our spirit cannot come forth, and the impression we leave will not be a spiritual one.

Suppose a brother is speaking about the Holy Spirit. Whereas his subject is the Holy Spirit, yet his words, his attitudes, and his illustrations are full of 'self.' Perhaps without his knowing why, the audience inwardly suffers while listening to him. His mouth is full of words about the Holy Spirit, but he leaves the impression of his self-life with his listeners. What is the spiritual value of such empty talk?

Rather than stressing teaching, let us place more emphasis on what it is that comes forth from us. God is not watching to see if our teaching becomes deeper or more advanced. He wants to lay hold of us as individuals. If our nature is not properly dealt with even though we may give forth so-called spiritual teaching, there is no spiritual impression or life-giving impartation. How tragic it is to impress others with the self-life of the outward man and not impart something of a living impression flowing from the inward man!

Again and again, God arranges our circumstances to break us of our self's natural strength. You may be stricken once, or twice, but still the third blow must come. God will not let you go. He will not stay His hand until He has broken your self's dominant characteristic.

What the Holy Spirit accomplishes through daily discipline is totally different from what happens when hearing a message. A message we hear may often remain in our minds for several months, possibly years, before its truth will become operative in us. The hearing often precedes the real entrance into life.

However, by means of the disciplining of the Holy Spirit, we more readily see the truth and thus possess it. How strange it is that we grasp the mere knowledge of a message much faster than the reality we learn through discipline! Once we hear it, we remember it. But we may be disciplined ten times and still wonder why. The day discipline accomplishes its purpose is the day you really **see** the truth and **enter** into its reality. So the work of the Holy Spirit is to **break**

you down on the one hand, and to **build you up** on the other. Your heart will then say: "Thanks be unto the Lord! Now I know that His disciplining hand, which has been upon me for these past five or ten years, has been just to break this strong natural trait of self in me."

The Amazing Work of Slaying through Enlightenment

Having considered the disciplinary working of the Holy Spirit, let us now see how He employs another means to deal with our outward man. Besides His **discipline**, there will be His **enlightenment**. Sometimes these two are used simultaneously and sometimes alternately. At times, the discipline delegated in our circumstances is aimed at leveling our dominant characteristic. At other times, God graciously shines upon us to enlighten us. The flesh, as we know it, lives hidden in darkness. Many works of the flesh are allowed to exist because they are not recognized by us as fleshly. Once His light reveals the flesh to us, we tremble, not daring to move.

We have especially observed this at times when the church is rich in the Word of God. When the ministry of His Word is strong, lacking no prophetic utterance, light breaks out clear and strong. In such light, you begin to realize that even your own condemnation of your pride is itself pride. In fact, your very own talking against your pride is now boastful. Hence, as soon as you see pride in the light, you are sure to say, "How disgusting! So this is what **my** pride is! How abhorrent and loathsome it now is to me!" Pride, when seen in the light of revelation, differs completely from the pride you usually talked about so easily. Enlightenment exposes your true condition. Immediately, it dawns upon you that you are ten thousand times worse than any of your preconceived notions about your proud self. Right then and there, your prideful heart, your self-importance, your stubborn flesh will wither away under this blazing light and die with no hope of survival.

What Impression Do We Give?

Whatever is revealed "in the light" is slain by it. This is most marvelous! We are not first enlightened and then with the passage of time gradually be brought into death. Instead, we fall down instantaneously at the coming of this decimating light. As the Holy Spirit enlightens, so are we instantly dealt with. Revelation, then, includes both **seeing** and **slaying**. It is God's unique way of dealing. Once the defilement of the self is really exposed, it cannot remain. Therefore, light both reveals and slays at the same time.

Being slain by the light is one of the greatest imperatives in Christian experiences. Paul had no time to run away from the roadside to kneel down before the light shined upon him. Instead, he **fell** immediately! He dropped instantly to the ground, right on the spot, without taking another step. Although he was naturally self-assertive and intensely self-confident, he reacted to the light by falling down, feeling somewhat dumbfounded, yet inwardly exposed. How effectual was this light when it struck him to the ground! Let us note that this happened immediately—all at once! We might assume that God first enlightens our understanding, and then leaves it up to us to work it out later, or to make changes gradually. That is not God's way.

God will always show us how hateful and corrupt we are in our 'self.' When the reality of this happens, our immediate response will be: "How repulsive! What a wretch I am! So dirtied! So despicable!" Once God reveals the true condition of the ugly self, it will always cause man to fall down as dead. Once a proud person has been truly enlightened, he cannot so much as make another attempt to be proud again. The effect of this enlightenment will permanently leave its mark upon him for the rest of his days. He will always be keenly sensitive to the hatefulness, helplessness, and hopelessness of his own self.

On the other hand, this time of enlightenment is also the time for believing—not for asking, but for humble worship. God follows the same principle in His saving us as He does afterwards in His working in us. When the radiant light of the gospel shines upon us, we do not pray: "Lord, I **beseech** You to be my Savior." To pray thus, even for days, would bring no assurance of salvation. Faith will simply say: "Lord, I **receive** You as my Savior." Instantly, salvation takes place! In like manner, as soon as God's shining light subsequently comes upon us in His further working in our Christian life (after salvation), we shall immediately and humbly prostrate ourselves under His light and by explicit faith tell the Lord: "Lord, I **accept** Your sentence. I **agree** with Your judgment." This will prepare us for more light.

In that hour of utter unveiling, even our most noble deeds, performed in His name and with love to Him, will somehow lose their luster. You will detect the meanest inclination in every one of your highest motives and best purposes. What you considered as wholly for God now appears to be riddled with self-centered ambitions. Appallingly, self seems to permeate every fragment of your being, robbing God of His glory.

To us it has seemed as if there is no depth of self to which man himself cannot plumb! Yet it takes God's revelation to expose prideful man in his deplorable condition. God will not stop until He lays us bare before our own eyes until we see ourselves. At first, He alone knows us, for we are always bare and naked **before Him**. But once God has disclosed to us the thoughts and intents of our heart, we are then laid bare **before ourselves**. How dare we lift up our head ever again? Leniency with ourselves becomes a thing of the past. Although we used to think of ourselves as better than others, now we know what we really are, and we are ashamed to show ourselves. We search in vain for words adequate enough to describe our loathsome and despicable condition. Our shame weighs heavily upon us, as if carrying the shame of the whole world. Feeling the anguish of Job, after we fall before the Lord and repent, we agonize: *"I abhor myself and repent in dust and ashes*—surely, I am incurable."

Such enlightenment, such self-abhorrence, such shame, such humiliation, and such repentance will deliver us from the self-centered bondage of long years. Once the Lord enlightens, He delivers instantly. Enlightenment is deliverance, and seeing is freedom. Only thus does our proud flesh cease to act, and our outward shell is broken.

Discipline Compared with Revelation

Let us make a comparison between this twofold work of the Holy Spirit—His discipline and His revelation. First of all, the discipline of the Holy Spirit is usually a slower process, being repeated time and again, perhaps for years, before the strong point at issue is finally dealt with. Incidentally, this discipline of the Holy Spirit oftentimes exists **without** any supply of ministry.

Not so with the revelation of the Holy Spirit. This often comes swiftly, within a few days, or possibly a few minutes. Under the searching light of God and within a very short period of time, you will see your proud, self-sufficient condition and discover how useless and washed-up you are. Here revelation frequently comes through the supply of God's Word. For this reason, the revelation of the Holy Spirit multiplies when the church is strong and the ministry of the Word is rich.

However, no one should imagine in the absence of such rich ministry and glowing revelation that he is then left free to live according to his outward man. It is important to remember that the discipline of the Holy Spirit still continues to be operative. Whereas one may be deprived of his contact with other believers for years, yet the presence of the Holy Spirit is always working within him. This is a great assurance to him, because this gives him encouragement for arriving at a matured spiritual state as long as he is inwardly responsive to the Spirit's discipline. While the weakness of the church may result in some members lacking the supply of God's Word, they have only themselves to blame if they miss the valuable significance of the Spirit's daily discipline. Moreover, their failure does not mean that the Holy Spirit has not or does not discipline them. Rather, it means that the years of discipline have produced no effect. Although the Lord has smitten once and again, they remained stubbornly ignorant of its meaning. Like a stubborn horse or mule void of understanding, they seem not to fathom the Lord's mind—even after ten years of His dealing. How pitiful is their lack of progress! We can only make this conclusion: Discipline is plentiful in many lives, but recognizing the hand of the Lord during those years of discipline is rare indeed.

How often when the Lord deals with us, we see only the outward hand of man. This is entirely wrong. Like the Psalmist, our attitude should be, *"I was dumb, I opened not my mouth, for Thou hast done it"* (Psalm 39:9). We must remember that **it is God** Who is behind all dealings, not our brother or sister or any other visible person.

Has the Lord disciplined us for many years, but instead of recognizing His hand, we blamed it on other people or on fate? Constantly, may we be reminded that **everything is measured by God for us.** He has predetermined its time, its boundary, and its intensity in order to break our hard-to-deal-with dominant characteristics. Oh, may we have the grace to recognize His hand and its meaning when He seeks to shatter our outward man! Until that happens, people will only meet our imperious self when they come in contact with us. Until the breaking is effected, our spirit cannot flow forth freely toward them.

Earnestly we pray that the church may know God as never before, that God's children may be increasingly fruitful unto Him. The Lord intends to bring us into the place where not only our Gospel message and teaching ministry are correct, but also the **person** behind the preaching and teaching is right as well. The challenging issue is this: Can God be fully released through our spirit?

When our spirit is released, it will supply the true needs of the world. No work is more important or more thorough than this—and nothing can take its place. The Lord is not so much concerned with

94

our teachings or sermons as He is with the impression we give. What is it that comes out of us—this is the final yardstick? Do we impress people with ourselves, or with the Lord? Do we draw people to our teaching, or to the Lord? This is genuinely vital. It determines the value of all our work and labor.

Beloved, be assured the Lord pays far more attention to what comes out of your life than what comes out of your mouth. Do not forget that in every contact you make with someone, something comes out of you. It is either the self coming out of your outward man or God Who is flowing forth out of your spirit. Explicitly, I would ask you again: When you stand before people, what is it that comes forth? And lest we are too quick to give an answer, let us remember that this basic question can only be properly answered **in His light.**

9

Meekness
in
Brokenness

GOD'S METHOD in breaking our outward man varies according to the **target**. Let us explain the target in this way: With some people, the target is their self-love. With others, it's their pride. Still others need their self-reliance and their cleverness to be targeted. The latter will find themselves in one predicament after another, defeated at every turn, until they, at long last, will learn to say, "We will live no longer in fleshly wisdom, but in God's grace." Moreover, those whose distinctive characteristic is subjective feelings will find themselves in circumstances peculiar to their need. And further, some brothers are always brimming over with ideas and opinions. The Lord in the Bible affirms, *"Is there anything*

97

too hard for Me?" (Jer. 32:27), but these brothers maintain that nothing is too hard for them! They boast that they can do everything. But eventually it is strange that they somehow fail in every undertaking. Things that before seemed so easy now fall apart in their hands. In their perplexity, they ask, "Why?" This is how the Holy Spirit deals with them in order to reach His necessary target. These illustrations show how each target of the Spirit varies according to each individual's condition.

There is, furthermore, a variation in the **tempo** of the Holy Spirit's dealings. At times the blows may swiftly follow one upon another without any reprieve. Or, there may be periods loaded with lulls. But all whom the Lord loves He disciplines, subdues, and corrects. Thus, God's children bear wounds inflicted by the Holy Spirit. While the external afflictions may vary, the outcome is the same—the self within is wounded and the will of the outward man is broken. So God touches our self-love, pride, cleverness, subjectivity—whatever constitutes His target. He intends by each blast at the target to weaken us further, until the day comes when our proud, inflexible will is crushed and made pliable in His hands. Whether His dealing touches our affections or our thoughts, the final result is to accomplish a broken will. We are all naturally obstinate. This hard, inflexible will is supported by our strong thoughts, opinions, self-love, affections, or cleverness. This explains the variations in the Holy Spirit's dealings with us. In the final analysis, God is after our will, for it is this which represents the self.

Thus, a common feature marks out those who have been enlightened and disciplined—they become meek. Meekness is the sign of brokenness. All who are broken by God are characterized by meekness. Formerly, we could afford to be inflexible and obstinate, because we were like a house well buttressed by many supporting walls. As God removes these walls one after another, the house is bound to collapse. When the supporting walls are toppled, the interior strength of self cannot but fall.

But we must learn to recognize true meekness. Do not be deceived into thinking that a soft-spoken voice indicates a gentle will. Often an iron will lies hidden behind the softest voice. Stubborn inflexibility is in the hidden nature of our character, not in the voice. Some appear outwardly to be more gentle **before others**, but they are inwardly just as inflexible and obstinate **before God**. For them, there can only be the severity of His dealing until they dare not act presumptuously. God designs external dealings to touch us at the core where our toughen wills hide out. Never shall we be able to raise our stubborn heads in these particular matters. It is irrevocably determined that in these kinds of circumstances, we cannot disobey the Lord by insisting upon our willful opinions. It is the fear of the Lord's dealing hand that restrains us. And it is the fear of God that makes us meek. The more we are broken by God's dealings, the meeker we become. To see true meekness is to behold inner brokenness.

Let us illustrate it in this way: After contacting a certain brother, you may sense that he is truly gifted. But you discover that he is yet unbroken. Many are like that—gifted, but not broken. Their unbrokenness and hardheartedness can be detected easily. As soon as you meet them, you sense an undertone of inflexibility in them. Not so with one who is broken—in him are the indications of a Spirit-wrought meekness. At whatever point wherein one has been chastened by God, therein he dares not to boast. He has learned to fear God in each prideful area, and his life is eventually transformed into meekness.

Please notice how the Scripture uses different metaphors to describe the Holy Spirit. He is like Fire, and He is also like Water. Fire speaks of His power. Water of His cleansing. But in reference to the nature of His character, He is said to be like a Dove—meek, lowly, and gentle. The Spirit of God will incorporate His nature into us little by little until we, too, are characterized by the Dove's nature.

Meekness, born out of the fear of God, is the Holy Spirit's sign for brokenness.

Considering the Qualities of Meekness

One broken by the Spirit inherently possesses meekness. His contacts with people are no longer marked by that temper and tone of inflexibility, harshness, and sharpness—the hallmarks of an unbroken man. He has been brought to the place where his attitude is as meek as his voice is gentle. The fear of God in his heart naturally finds expression in his words and viewpoints.

1— Easily Approachable

There are several qualities which characterize a person who is meek. First, he is approachable. He is so easily available for contact, fellowship, and inquiries. He confesses his sin readily and sheds tears freely. How difficult it is for some to shed tears. It is not that there is any special value in tears, but in one whose thought, will, and emotions have been dealt with by God, tears often denote his readiness to see his faults and to acknowledge his mistakes. He is easy to talk with, for his outward shell has been broken. Open to the opinions of others, he welcomes instructions, and in this new attitude he is receptive to be edified in all things.

2—Highly Sensitive

Again, one who is meek is alert to the spiritual atmospheres of the Lord's people. Because his spirit can easily come forth, he can touch the spirit within his brethren. The slightest movement in the spirit of others does not go by him unnoticed. Almost immediately, he can detect the true spiritual significance of a situation—regardless of whether it is right or wrong. Whatever the circumstances, his spirit is readily responsive. His actions are insightful. And he will never inconsiderately be offensive to the feelings of others.

Too often we persist in doing things which the spirit of others have already disapproved. This indicates that our outward man is not broken. Others are especially sensitive about it, but we remain insensitive and numb. Consider how this may occur in our prayer meetings, when the brothers and sisters may feel some inner distastefulness toward our prayers. Yet we drone on and on. The spirits of the other brethren have inwardly come forth—not verbally—and in essence crying out, "Stop your praying!" But we remain insensitive. We have no inner responsiveness to the feelings of others. Not so with the one whose outward man has been broken. Because the Spirit has wrought a deep sensitivity, intuitively he touches, and can be touched by, the spiritual sense of others. Such a one will not be dull or insensitive to the spiritual reactions of others.

3—Mutually Corporate

Only the broken ones know meaningfully what is the reality of the Body of Christ. Without meekness, people can hardly be ready for a participation of a corporate life with other believers. Only the meek, broken brothers can begin to touch the corporate spirit of the Body, and be even considerate of the spiritual feelings of other members. If one lacks this Body feeling, he is like a numbed, paralyzed member of the body. Or, like an artificial hand which may move mechanically in the physical body, but without any feeling. The whole Body has a corporate sense of the spirit in the members, but not him. Neither can he meekly receive guidance or adjustment. However, a member whose outer man is broken can touch the conscience of the church and know the mutual feelings of the church. Why? Because his released spirit is open to the common spirit in the church, and the church can easily impart fellowship to his open spirit.

How precious is this mutual spiritual sensitivity! Whenever we are wrong, we sense it immediately. Although we are not freed from making mistakes, we possess nonetheless a faculty in our spirit which will quickly prick us. Brothers and sisters who are related to us know early when we make a mistake. Even before they open up their mouths, we already know it because we are brought to the same inner sense. Simply by an initial contact with them, we have instantly touched their spirit and know something is wrong. Spiritual signals from the released spirit found in the Body have indicated approval or disapproval. It becomes evident that meekness, which is the fruit of brokenness, is a basic requirement, and without it, a corporate Body-life is impossible.

The Body of Christ lives in the same way as our physical body. It does not require the calling of a general committee in order to reach decisions. Nor is there need for prolonged discussions. All of the members naturally and organically possess a common feeling, and that feeling expresses the mind of the Body. And what is more significant, it is also the expression of the mind of the Head. Therefore, the mind of the Head is known through the spirit of the Body. This spirit is also called the inner consciousness of the inner anointing—the inner flow of the released spirit. After our outward man is broken, we begin to mutually live in that corporate awareness, which is only possible through the released spirit of related members in His Body. Consequently, we are easily calibrated.

4—Spiritually Receptive

The greatest advantage of brokenness, however, is not in having our mistakes corrected, but rather in enabling us to receive openly and freely the life supply from other members of the Body. One whose spirit is released is open to get spiritual help from whatever spiritual source is available among the members of the Body. But one who is not broken can hardly receive help.

Suppose, for example, a brother has a brilliant but unbroken intellect. He may come to the meetings of a local church, but he is untouched. Unless he meets someone whose mind is sharper than his, he will not be helped. He will analyze the thoughts of the preacher and reject them as useless and meaningless. Months and years may pass by, and it is impossible for anything to touch his spirit. His spirit is stonewalled by his intellectual mind. Because of this mental impediment, it would seem as if he could only be helped through his mentality. In this kind of condition he cannot receive spiritual edification. However, should the Lord come in and shatter this wall, showing him the futility of his own intellectual mind, he will then become simple like a child and listen attentively to what others may be saying. He will no longer despise people who seem to be inferior to his capabilities or capacities.

While listening to a message, we should use our spirit to contact the spirit of the preacher, rather than focusing upon the correct pronunciation of his words or on the rambling presentation of his doctrines. When the spirit of the preacher is released with a definite word from the Lord, our spirit is refreshed and edified. If our spirit is free and open, we will receive help whenever a brother's spirit is released and flows forth. But remember, this is not the same as being helped doctrinally. The more thoroughly the outward man is broken and the more spontaneously a man's spirit is flowing, the greater help he is spiritually able to receive. And it is also true that whenever God's Spirit makes a move upon any brother, never again will he judge others merely by doctrines, words, or eloquence. His attitude is entirely changed. Here is an invariable principle: The measure of help we can receive from others depends upon the openness of our spirit.

103

Now we must clearly understand what is meant by being spiritually edified. It cannot mean the progressive development of thoughts, nor an increased improvement of understanding, nor a greater accumulation of doctrinal truth. Spiritual edification simply means that my spirit has once more been in fresh contact with God's Spirit. It does not matter through whom or in what place—whether in the meeting or in individual fellowship—as long as the Spirit of God is moving, I am nonetheless nourished and revived. My spirit, whenever it beholds and reflects the divine Spirit, is always edified and refreshed (2 Cor. 3:18). Like a mirror that is always bright and shining by constant polishing, so my spirit is always bright and shining by a constant contact with the released spirit of other believers, through whom the life-giving Spirit flows.

Suppose we explain it like this: Whatever proceeds from a released spirit brightens everything it reaches. As individuals, we are very much like light bulbs—different colored light bulbs. Yet the color does not interfere with the electricity passing through it. As soon as the electricity flows into it, it lights up. So is it with our spirit. When there is the flowing energy of His Spirit, we will forget about having our heads full of bookish knowledge. All we know is that the liberating Spirit has freely come. Instead of mere cerebral knowledge, we have a bright, shiny, life-giving 'inner light.' What emerges is that we are freshly revived and sufficiently nourished in His presence.

Beforehand, our scholarly intellectualism has made it impossible to receive spiritual edification, but now we can easily be helped. Now we understand why it is hard for others to receive help. We understand that it requires spending much time in prayer before we can touch them with a released spirit where there is spiritual edification. There is no other way to help a headstrong person. As we shall see in the next lesson, there is a way God has designed for true effectiveness.

10

Two Very
Different Ways

WE MUST RECOGNIZE two very different ways of help before us. First, *"there is a way that **seemeth** right"* in which help is received from the outside—by external doctrines and expositions, making their appeal to the mind. Many will even profess to having been greatly helped by this way. Yet, this outward help is so very different from the inward help which God really intends.

Second, we must see that God's true way of help is the inward way of **spirit touching spirit**. Instead of having our mentality developed or acquiring a storehouse of knowledge, life is received and we are edified by the contact of the inner spirit. Let no one be

105

deceived. Unless we have found this way, we have not found true Christianity. This alone is the way of having our inward man edified or built up.

Let us present it like this: If you are accustomed to sermons, undoubtedly it would annoy you to hear the same message from the same preacher twice. You might feel certain it is enough to hear the message once. This is because your conception of Christianity is simply doctrinal—the storing of correct knowledge in your mind. Do you not realize that spiritual edification is not a question of doctrine, but of touching each other's spirit? If a member speaks through his spirit, you will feel clean and fresh each time his spirit comes out and touches you, regardless of the familiarity of the subject or the frequency of hearing the same theme repeatedly. Any teaching or doctrine which does not result in reviving the spirit can only be considered as a dead letter.

Moreover, there is something quite remarkable about someone who is broken. If you are one who is indeed broken, you will discover that you are not only able to give spiritual help, but while giving it, you also receive spiritual help simultaneously. For example, someone asks you a question. And in answering it, you are inwardly helped. You pray with a sinner who is seeking the Lord. And again your prayer inwardly strengthens you. You may be led to speak decisively with a brother who has slipped. Not only is his spirit thereby revived, but you too are inwardly refreshed. In other words, you are able to receive some life-edifying help from every spiritual contact you make. You marvel how the whole Body is able to supply you as a functioning member. Any member of the Body can supply your need, and as a result you are strengthened. You become a recipient of the supply richly contained in the Body. How rich and how sweet it is! You can truly rejoice: "The wealth of the Head belongs to the Body, and the wealth of the Body belongs to me as a member!" How greatly this differs from the mere delivery of mental knowledge!

This ability of receiving help—allowing the spirit of others to touch our spirit—is proof that one is broken. It takes more than merely our cleverness to make it difficult for us to receive help. Rather, it is symptomatic of a hard outer shell. In the Lord's mercy, a strong, clever person must be dealt with drastically and be broken many times and in many ways. Then, one day, he is receptive to the supply of the whole church. Let us ask ourselves: "Are we receptive to the supply flowing from others?" If we cannot receive edification from others, it is likely that a thick shell of our outward man is preventing us from touching their released spirit. But if we are broken, as soon as their spirit flows, we receive help. The question is, then, not how powerful is someone's individual spirit, but has his spirit circulated in the Body and touched the spirit of every member? This mutual flowing of everyone's spirit in the members of the Body is what revives and builds each other up. What a necessity it is then for the outward man to be broken. There can be no question but that this breaking constitutes the basic requirement for both giving help and receiving help.

Fellowship of the Believers' Spirits

Spiritual fellowship is much more than the meeting of the minds or an exchange of ideas and opinions. True fellowship is the mutual interaction of the released spirit flowing from the members of the Body. This kind of fellowship is possible only after our outward man has been shattered, and our spirit is henceforth released to touch the spirit of others. In this reciprocal sharing of our spirit with one another, we experience the real fellowship of the saints. Then we understand what the Scriptures mean by the *"fellowship of the Spirit"* (Phil. 2:1). Truly, it is an interflow of fellowship between the Spirit and our spirits, and not merely an interchange of ideas. It is by this fellowship with one another's spirit that we can pray in one accord.

Because many pray through their minds, independent of their spirits, it is difficult for these believers to find others of the same mind who can pray in one accord with them.

Anyone who is born anew and has the Holy Spirit indwelling his regenerated spirit can have fellowship with us. This is only made possible when our spirit is open for some mutual fellowship with all believers. We are ready both to receive our brother's spirit and to let him receive our spirit. This is how we can touch the Body of Christ, for we are all parts of the Body. Can we comprehend it when we say that our spirits, added together collectively, are the Body of Christ? The Body of Christ is something in the realm of the spirit of all believers. Indeed, *"deep calleth unto deep"* (Ps. 42:7). The *"deep"* refers to the liberated release of our human spirit. The **deep** of your spirit is calling for a touch with the **deep** of my spirit. And we all are calling for a touch with the **deep** of the whole church. Herein is the mutual fellowship of the '**deeps**,' the calling and the answering of the **deep** with one another. This is the one thing most necessary if we are to be useful before the Lord and properly touch the released spirit of the church.

A Meekness Beyond Imitation

When we suggest that it is essential for us to be meek, we are not trying to persuade you to act meek. For if you do, you will soon discover that this man-made effort of meekness needs to be shattered. We must learn once and for all that any human striving to imitate meekness is futile. Meekness must issue from the work of the Holy Spirit, for **He alone** knows our need and will arrange circumstances leading to the breaking of our outward man.

It is our responsibility first to ask God for enough light to recognize the mighty hand of the Holy Spirit, then to submit to it willingly, and finally to acknowledge that whatever He does is His prerogative. Let us not be as mules without understanding. Rather, let us hand ourselves over to **the Lord alone** for Him to work in us. As you give yourself to the Lord, you will discover that His work actually began five or ten years earlier, though it seemingly has not yet produced any fruit in you. Today, a change has come. Finally, you can pray, "Lord, I was blind-folded, not knowing how You were leading me. But now I see that You wanted to break me. For this, I surrender myself to You." All that was unfruitful for the past five or ten years will eventually begin to bear fruit. We find the Lord is skillfully moving in to break many of the things we were totally unaware of. This is the work of His masterpiece: To deprive us of our pride, self-love, and self-exaltation. And to liberate our spirit until it finds its life fully exercised and its service wholly useful.

Two Related Questions

Two questions arise here for us to consider. Since the breaking of the outward man is the work of the Holy Spirit in defying man's imitation, should we try to stop any fleshly motion or gesture we recognize? Or must we acquiescently wait until greater light comes from the Holy Spirit, knowing that He is the Doer of the work?

Surely it is right and proper to stop every activity of the flesh. But we must see how vastly different this is from imitating the Spirit's work. Let's illustrate: Although I tend to be proud, I must refuse all pride. But I should not fabricate or mimic humility. Moreover, I am apt to lose my temper with people, and I should keep it under control. But I should not pretend to have gentleness. As long as my negative temper is struggling to break out, I should resist it without letup. Nevertheless, I should not pretend to have any of these genuine virtues, because any pretense is a counterfeit.

In other words, here is an important distinction: Pride as a negative thing is something I can deal with, but humility as a positive thing is something I should not imitate. Yes, I must put a stop to all fleshly activities known to me, but I do not need to emulate any of the positive virtues. All I need to do is to commit myself to the Lord, saying: "Lord, there is no reason for me to exert my effort to imitate any virtues. I am trusting You to do the work."

Man's imitation is never God's work, and it is always from man's effort. All who seek the Lord must learn to cooperate with the Spirit within, not just to conform outwardly by the energies of the soul. We must allow God to finish His work **within** us before we can expect the fruit of His work to be manifested **without**. Whatever is manufactured outwardly by our own effort is not real and is doomed to frustration and defeat. One who has unwittingly possessed a counterfeit characteristic defrauds others as well as himself. As counterfeit behavior develops, the person deceives himself into believing that such performance is his real self. It is often perplexing to convince him of his illusion and aberration, for he cannot distinguish the true from the false. Therefore, we must never try to imitate outward virtues. It is far better for us to be spontaneous and unaffected. This opens the way for God to work in us. Let us be simple and not imitate anything, having confidence in the Lord Himself to manifest His virtues through us.

The second question is that since some people are naturally endowed with such virtues as gentleness, is there a difference between their natural gentleness and the gentleness which comes through the Spirit's discipline?

There are two points to be considered in answering this question. First, recognize that natural virtues are independent of the spirit, while the virtues which come through the discipline of the Holy Spirit are under our spirit's control and find expression only as our spirit moves. Furthermore, natural gentleness may be a hindrance to the spirit. One who is habitually gentle is gentle in himself, not *"in the Lord."* Suppose the Lord wants him to stand up and utter some strong words. His natural gentleness will hinder him from following the Lord. He

110

would say instead, "Oh! This I cannot do! I have never in my life uttered such hard words. Let someone else do it. I just simply cannot do it!" So now you can see how his natural gentleness is not under his spirit's control. Anything that is natural has its own will and acts independent of the spirit. However, the gentleness which comes through brokenness can be used by his spirit. It does not have its own opinions and is not resistant to and independent of the control of his spirit.

Second, a naturally gentle person is only gentle only as long as you are going along with his will. If you force him to do what he does not like to do, he will change his attitude and become more inflexible. Lacking in all of the so-called human virtues is the element of self-denial. Obviously, the instinctive purpose of all these natural virtues and values is to build up and strengthen the self-life. When a man's self is infringed upon, all of his human virtues will disappear. The virtues which spring from spiritual discipline, on the other hand, are only produced after our ugly self-life has been conquered. The place where God is breaking the self is the place where true virtue is seen. The more the strength of self is wounded, the brighter shines the true gentleness. So natural virtues, then, are basically different from the fruit of the Spirit.

A Final Exhortation

Having stressed the importance of the breaking of the outward man, let us be careful lest we try to effect this artificially. We must clearly submit ourselves under the mighty hand of God and simply accept all of God's allotted and necessary dealings. As the outward man is severely broken, the inward man is strengthened. A few however may still find the inward man still feeble after such relentlessly breaking experiences. Therefore, do not **pray** for strength to rectify yourself just because the Bible commands you to "be strong." But **proclaim** that it is your purpose and intention to be strong. The marvelous thing is, after your outward man is broken, that you can be strong whenever you want to be strong. The issue of strength is resolved when the problem of the outward man is resolved. Consequently, you can be strong when you want to be strong. Nothing can block the release of your spirit. Once the Lord tells you to *"Be strong,"* with boldness you can also decide to say, I will *"Be strong in the Lord!"* And you will discover how the Lord is your strength.

> *"We should, we must, we can, we will,*
> *Fulfill God's purpose faithfully."*

In conclusion, the inward man is freed only after the outward man is broken. This is the basic road to blessing in the Lord's service.

Study Guide

for

The Release
of
the Spirit

Published by

Sure Foundation Publishers

Study Guide
for
The Release of the Spirit

Preface

1. What was the Author's major purpose in writing this book? (Read page 5)

2. How does Satan work? (Page 5)

3. What is imperative if we are going to express the life of the Lord Jesus? (Page 6)

Introduction

1. Describe the terminology used by the Author for the three parts of man. (Page 7)

2. Where does God dwell, and why? (Page 7)

3. If God is to govern man's soul through the Holy Spirit's indwelling of his spirit, what must first take place? Illustrate

114

this by Jacob's life in Genesis. (Page 8)

4. Why does the Author insist on the breaking and mastering of the soul, the outer man? (Pages 8-9)

Chapter 1: The Importance of Brokenness

1. Describe how the outward man (soul) and the inward man (spirit) are not in harmony. (Page 11)

2. From four references (Rom. 7:22; Eph. 3:16; 2 Cor. 4:16; 1 Cor. 6:17), show how the Bible divides man into two parts, helping thus to illustrate man's three parts by clothing. (Page 12)

3. What is the basic failure of believers seeking to serve God? (Page 13)

4. From John 12:24-25, how does nature characterize this profound principle of breaking? Who is this grain of wheat? (Pages 13-14)

5. From Mark 14:3, how does the alabaster box confirm this principle of breaking? (Pages 14-15)

6. How does the Holy Spirit break the outward man? (Page 15)

7. From 2 Corinthians 4:7-12, how does Paul authenticate the Lord's purpose of brokenness? (Pages 15-16)

8. Explain how the Lord will employ two time-methods to break our outward man. (Pages 16-17)

9. What is the true meaning of the cross in the light of breaking our soulishness for the release of our spirit? (Pages 17-18)

10. What two reasons does the Author give to explain why it takes years to break the strong hindrances of our outward man? (Pages 18-19)

11. How did Jacob encounter brokenness, and what were the results of his experiences ? (Pages 20-21)

12. In your own life, what unbroken part of your outward man (soul) tends to be the strongest? Name specific things of mind (thoughts), emotions (feelings), and will (choices). Ask God for light to help you answer this question.

13. List specific life situations, circumstances, and trials which God has brought into your life recently to break down one of your stubborn soul-strengths you listed under question 12.

Chapter 2: Before and After Brokenness

1. How does the unbroken self, which weakens our service to God, affect the condition of our human spirit? Name two conditions. (Page 23)

2. Using John 6:63 and 1 Corinthians 3:6, explain how the Spirit

joined to our spirit (1 Cor. 6:17) makes our work for the Lord more effective. (Page 24)

3. Explain why the divine Spirit and the human spirit are uniquely separable and yet not so easily distinguishable? (Pages 24-25)

4. How does the Divine Spirit employ the human spirit? (Page 25)

5. Why is a man's usefulness more dependent upon his outward man than on his human spirit? (Page 25)

6. What are some of the practical problems in preaching, teaching, testifying, or witnessing where harmony between the outward man and the inward man is lacking? Name two contrastive dilemmas. (Pages 26-27)

7. How does the release of our human spirit depend upon the cooperation of the thoughts, emotions, and will of the outward man? (Page 27)

8. What causes the practice of the Presence of God to be such a frustrating experience to most believers? Refer to John 4:24 in your answer. (Pages 28-29)

9. Once the outward man of the soul is broken, describe how the inner man can maintain his enjoyment of God's Presence—in spite of compelling interests (curiosity), emotional outbursts of love and anger, distracting circumstances and events, running errands, doing menial tasks, being pulled by engaging activities, conversing with people, or dealing with the faults of others. (Pages 29-32)

10. The dividing of the outward man (soul) from the inward man

(spirit) defines the problem of the outward influencing the inward. What is the problem, and give two examples of a divided daily life? (Pages 32-33)

11. According to the Author's definition, are you a single or a dual person? (Page 33)

12. The ability to use our spirit as God intends depends upon what two-fold work of God? (Page 34)

Chapter 3: Recognizing "The Thing In Hand"

1. Explain the Author's subject of "the thing in hand"? (Page 35) List "the things in hand" surrounding your life which occupy your soul.

2. How does our limited human strength—mentally, emotionally, and volitionally—render the law of the Spirit of life ineffectual? (Pages 36-37) What area in your life is the most limiting thing which occupies you, and why?

3. What is a very important principle to grasp in order to be an available outlet for God's Spirit? Name three things which block the flow through the channel of life. (Page 38)

4. How does God deal with our "things in hand"? (Pages 38-39)

5. How does a unified personality of an unsaved person compare to that of an unbroken believer? How can this condition be

reversed? (Page 40)

6. Why do right teachings fail to transform a vessel fit for the Master's use? (Page 41)

7. What is one immutable law of God's purpose by which God works in our lives? Can prayer change this law? (Page 42)

Chapter 4: How to Know Man

1. What does the Author mean by "knowing man," and why is it so important? (Page 43)

2. What happens when you use your independent mind and personal feelings to discern a person's spiritual condition? (Page 44)

3. Why can we not depend upon what an individual tells us about his own spiritual complaints? (Page 44)

4. Even with God's Spirit working through us, can we know the spiritual condition of everyone who comes to us? What then should we do, and why? (Page 45)

5. Why is it that we cannot discern or diagnose what "ails" a person spiritually? (Pages 46-47)

6. What are the two ways that God's Spirit uses to meet needs and solve problems among His people? (Pages 47-48)

7. Since our human spirit emanated from God and is designed to manifest the Spirit of God, how is it possible, then, for man's spirit to be spoken of as being proud, sad, hasty, hard, haughty, depressed, unforgiving, and jealous?
   (Pages 48-49)

8. What are the two sides for knowing man as "God's patient"?
   (Pages 48-50)

9. What kind of lesson must be learned in order to serve? For how long and to what degree? (Pages 50-51)

10. How do we practice releasing our spirit in order to pinpoint the real conditions of others? (Page 52)

11. When brothers argue about what's right or wrong, what must we listen for while dealing with their problem? (Pages 53-54)

Chapter 5:   The Church and God's Work

1. Compare and make contrasts about how God manifests His work in both Christ and the church. (Pages 55-57)

2. Explain why *what we are* determines *what we get* out of Bible reading. (Page 57)

3. What are the two basic requirements for reading the Bible?
   (Page 58)

4. How does breaking the mind of the outward man help us to enter into the thought of God's Word? (Page 58)

5. What is the most outstanding feature of the Bible, and how do we connect with it practically? (Page 59)

6. What does "the ministry of the Word" mean? (Pages 59-60)

7. Why is it difficult to release the Word from our spirit, and how is this characterized? (Page 60)

8. What are the two common misconceptions in preaching the Gospel, and how should the Gospel be preached? (Pages 61-63)

9. How should people be saved normally, as seen in the Gospels and Acts? (Pages 62-63)

Chapter 6: Brokenness and Discipline

1. What two things are imperative for the breaking of the outward man, and how are these two things portrayed? (Page 65)

2. What is the vital distinction between consecration and discipline? (Page 66)

3. What are the two phases of the Holy Spirit working in our lives? (Pages 66-67)

4. Why does God use external things and why does He order our circumstances to deal with our outward man? (Pages 67-68)

5. Why is consecration to the Lord so important for His working in our lives? (Page 68)

6. List several means of grace; then, state the greatest means of grace? (Page 69)

7. Explain how the Holy Spirit will discipline the following areas where the soulish life dominates your outward man—material things, relationships, thought life, uncontrollable emotions, stubborn self-will, self-assertive judgments, opinions and excuses, and the insufficient supply of God's Word. Which one is the strongest in your life, and how do you recognize the Spirit's disciplining hand? (Pages 70-73)

8. Among the following, which one meets our need the most, and why—the supply of God's Word, the power of prayer, the encouragement of fellowship, or the discipline of the Holy Spirit? (Pages 72-73)

9. How is the daily operation of the cross related to the discipline of the Holy Spirit? (Page 73)

Chapter 7: Dividing and Revelation

1. What does God want to do besides breaking down our outward man? Explain why. (Pages 75-76)

2. How does God accomplish the dividing and the breaking down? (Page 76)

3. Does the dividing go further than the release of the Spirit? Explain why. (Pages 76-77)

4. Explain why the impurity of mixtures is a major problem in the lives of God's servants? (Page 77)

5. Among God's children, which one of the Holy Spirit's work comes first—the breaking by His discipline or the dividing by His revelation? (Page 78)

6. What is meant by the phrase in Hebrews 4:12-13, *"the Word of God is living and operative"*? Illustrate how the Word from John 3:16 can become *"living and operative."* Illustrate it with another verse from your own experience. (Pages 78-79)

7. What will the living, operative Word do for us? (Page 79)

8. What does God's Word discern, and how does its light effectuate a dividing of our soul from our human spirit? Give examples. (Pages 80-83)

9. From Hebrews 4:13, show the standard or criterion for the dividing light of the Spirit's revelation. Give examples of how this enlightenment operates to divide our soul and spirit. (Pages 83-86)

Chapter 8: What Impression Do We Give

1. What affects our testimony and service for the Lord more than our words or actions? Explain why. (Page 87)

2. Recount the Shunammite's impression of Elisha in 2 Kings 4 (Page 88)

3. List the impressions the Author gives which characterize the unbroken strengths of the outward man. (Pages 87-88)

4. What should be stressed more than spoken messages and teachings? Explain why. (Pages 89-90)

5. Describe "The Amazing Work of Slaying through Enlightenment." How did this impact the lives of both Paul and Job? (Pages 90-92)

6. What is the major difference between discipline and the revelation of the Holy Spirit? (Pages 93-94)

7. On what do we usually blame God's dealings? (Page 94)

8. What two things coming forth out of us determine the value of our work? (Page 95)

Chapter 9: Meekness in Brokenness

1. How does God's method vary in the breaking of our outward man according to His target? List illustrations. (Pages 97-98)

2. What is, in the final analysis, God's goal, and why? (Page 98)

3. What common feature is characterized by those who are enlightened, disciplined, and broken, and how do we recognize it? (Pages 98-99)

4. Describe the different metaphors of the Holy Spirit, and indicate which one is the sign for brokenness. (Pages 99-100)

5. What are the four qualities of the meekness of a broken man? List several characteristics describing each disposition of brokenness. (Pages 100-103)

6. What qualities emerge from the human spirit of a broken and meek person? (Pages 103-104)

7. What areas in your own outer man has God revealed to you that lack brokenness and meekness?

Chapter 10:   Two Very Different Ways

1. Characterize the contrast of these two very different ways of help. (Pages 105-106)

2. In the mutual life of the Body of Christ, what is the proof of brokenness in a member? (Pages 106-107)

3. What is the true spiritual fellowship among the members of the Body of Christ? By contrast, how does the participation differ among unbroken members? (Pages 107-108)

4. How do we avoid imitating a meekness induced by our self-effort? (Page 108)

5. Should we try to stop our fleshly actions, or should we wait passively until greater light comes from the Holy Spirit? (Pages 108-111)

6. Explain and illustrate how we can stop our fleshly activities and at the same time prevent an imitation of positive virtues. (Pages 109-110)

7. What is the difference between gentleness endowed naturally and gentleness produced spiritually through the discipline of the Holy Spirit? Consider two points in answering this question. (Pages 110-111)

8. What are the two opposite ways of praying for strength—one by the outward man and the other by the inward man? (Pages 111-112)